Arthur Evans Moule

The Glorious Land

Short Chapters on China, and Missionary Work There

Arthur Evans Moule

The Glorious Land
Short Chapters on China, and Missionary Work There

ISBN/EAN: 9783744661423

Printed in Europe, USA, Canada, Australia, Japan

Cover: Foto ©Andreas Hilbeck / pixelio.de

More available books at **www.hansebooks.com**

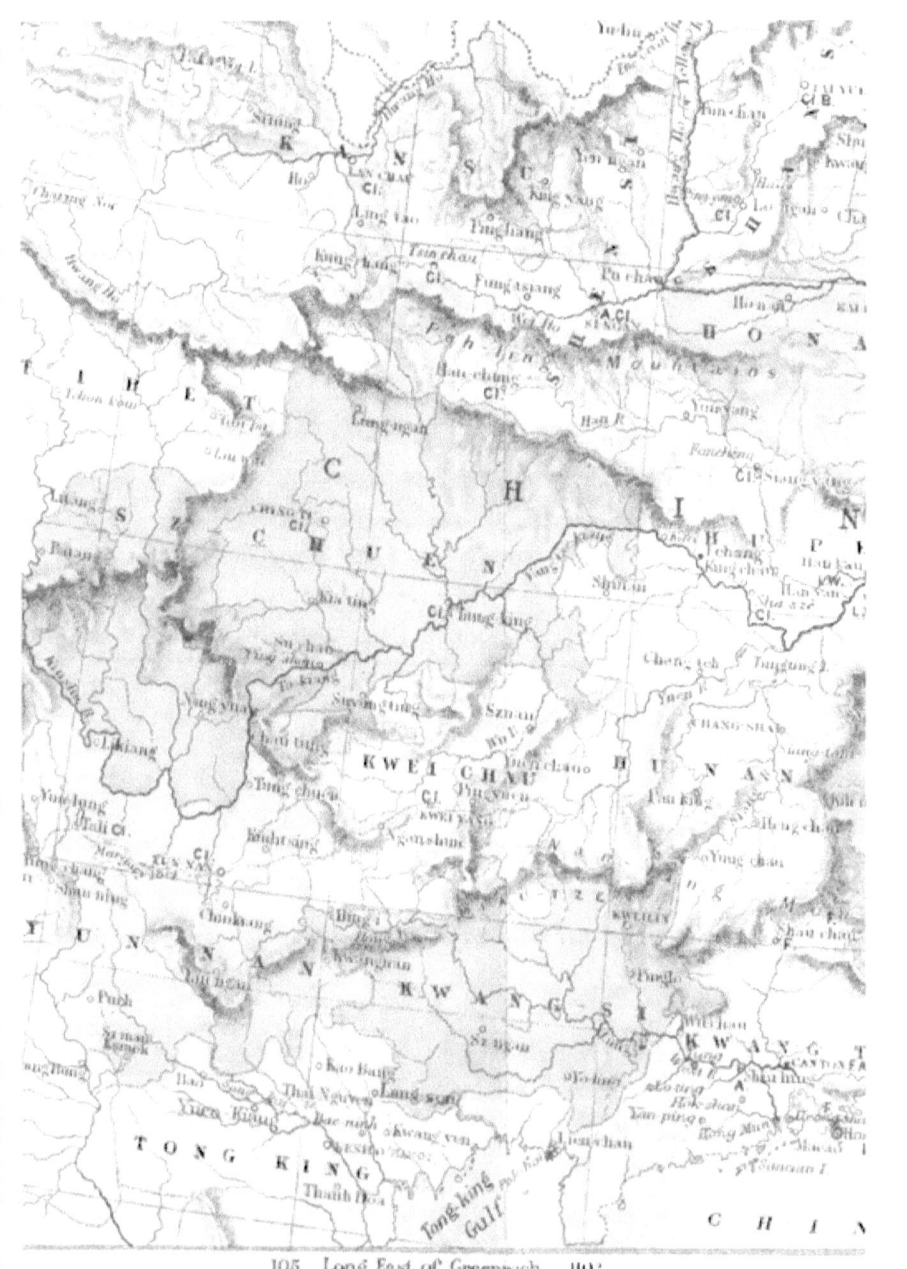

The Glorious Land.

SHORT CHAPTERS ON CHINA, AND MISSIONARY WORK THERE

BY THE

VEN. ARTHUR E. MOULE, B.D.,

Archdeacon in Mid-China, and Missionary of the C.M.S. in Ningpo, Hangchow, and Shanghai; Author of "The Story of the Cheh-Kian Mission," "Chinese Stories," "China as a Mission Field," etc.

WITH MAP AND ILLUSTRATIONS.

London:
CHURCH MISSIONARY SOCIETY,
SALISBURY SQUARE, E.C.

1891.

LONDON:
PRINTED BY PERRY, GARDNER AND CO.,
FARRINGDON ROAD, E.C.

PREFACE.

Two calls, like trumpet notes, have recently startled the Churches in Christendom; the one a demand for at least a thousand new workers to be sent within the next five years to China; the other an appeal specially addressed to the Church Missionary Society to send a thousand new labourers speedily into all heathen and Mahomedan lands. China monopolises the first appeal, which was one result of the great Mission Conference held last May in Shanghai; and China claims a large share in the second appeal, which was one result of the recent Keswick Convention. It is to emphasize these appeals that this small book has been written. May God use it to His glory, in the hastening of His kingdom! Meanwhile, louder and clearer and more persuasive far than human appeal, should not our Lord's command and promise be ever ringing in our ears,—the very last words of that beloved voice which fell on this lower air as He ascended up:—" Go, teach all nations. Lo! I am with you always."

CONTENTS.

		PAGE
CHAPTER I.—THE GLORIOUS LAND		7
,, II.—THE GREAT REBELLION		13
,, III.—THE GREAT REBELLION—THE STORM GOING DOWN		23
,, IV.—THE GREAT REBELLION—AFTERMATH OF THE HARVEST OF WOE		31
,, V.—FLOOD AND FAMINE		41
,, VI.—RELIGIOUS THOUGHT IN CHINA		51
,, VII.—FOUR SCENES IN CHINESE EVANGELIZATION		69
,, VIII.—UNEXPECTED AGENCIES		85
,, IX.—CHINA OPEN—THE FUTURE		95
,, X.—ALTER EGO—A WAKING DREAM		105

THE GLORIOUS LAND.

CHAPTER I.

THE GLORIOUS LAND.

CHINA was first seen by me early in August, 1861. One hundred days of baffling calms, of howling cyclones, and of strong fair trade winds, had brought us in the good ship *Solent* from the Downs to the Straits of Formosa. As the light airs above and the uncertain currents below drifted us to and fro, we caught glimpses of the far-off coast sleeping under the hot summer sun. Presently we ran amongst a large fleet of fishing-boats with five or six men in each, and with eager interest we watched these specimens of the race to which God, we trusted, had sent us. Soon we sighted the prominent Island of Video; and then with a long tack eastwards we caught the monsoon again, and sailed with half a gale of wind round the Saddle Islands and the Chusan Archipelago, and, picking up a pilot, we reached at last Woosung and Shanghai, 111 days from port to port. What was this great land like whose bare and rocky coast we had seen from afar; and whose rich alluvial plains round the mouths of the River Yangtse now caught our gaze; flat and featureless save for the brilliant green of the rice-fields and the darker hues of the cotton crop, and the willows and bushes lining the countless water-courses?

Twenty-nine years have passed since then, and my acquaintance with the country and the people makes me wonder less and less at the title given to China by the Chinese, " The Glorious or Brilliant Land." China is often called the Flowery Land. This is not exactly a misnomer, for the hills and plains of China are fair and fragrant with both wild and garden flowers. The chrysanthemum and the peony; the *olea fragrans* (changing for a few short weeks the air, heavy with the evil odours of earth, into the sweetness of Eden); the azalea, red and yellow, covering the hills for thousands of miles; the sheets of wild but almost scentless white and blue and red violets carpeting the banks of river and canal, all these belong to China. But they are not sufficient to give her the distinctive name of the Flowery Land; for European wild flowers are sweeter and fairer than those of China, and the Himalayas are more bowery and beautiful than Chinese hills. Her true name is rather the Glorious Land; the same word in Chinese meaning both flowery and glorious. And glorious the land is indeed, with its wide boundaries and enormous area. The region of Western China alone, that magnificent new world now fast opening to exploration and commerce, a region comprising the three provinces of Szchuen, Yunnan, and Kweichow, is larger by 20,000 square miles than Great Britain, Ireland, and France, and contains 80,000,000 inhabitants. The gigantic uplands of Thibet, from which the rivers Brahmaputra, Irawaddy, Mekong, Seluen, and Yangtse all take their rise, own China's supremacy; and the "roof of the world" in Nepaul is in theory, at any rate, under China's jurisdiction. Her outer rim is as long in mileage as the overland route from North China to England. Glorious she is in her great rivers and streams; in her mountain ranges; in her fruitful plains; in her countless walled cities and towns (though these look fairer far from a distance than on nearer inspection); glorious in her love of literature, and in her promotion of education. Glorious, too, may China be called in her history. She rose into life and power before all the other great monarchies of the world; she has outlived them all; and now in her extreme old age she is renewing her strength, and is destined to form one of the great triumvirate, the Anglo-Saxon race, the Russian, and the Chinese, which before the next century has gone far on its course, will perhaps divide the whole world.

It is one of the most interesting features of China's history to notice how civilised she became at an early period; how stationary or retrograde she has been since then; and how now, during the last years of the nineteenth century, she is slowly but with increasing momentum opening her gates for the entrance of

European science and civilisation. It is hard to believe that the city of Hangchow (not one of China's most ancient cities it is true, but founded 1,300 years ago, and with temples dating from 1,600 years back) became famous in the distant West before the close of the Middle Ages; European merchants, travellers, and missionaries having come to view it. Marco Polo, born about A.D. 1250, describes it as "without doubt the noblest and finest city in the world." The great street was paved throughout with stone slabs perfectly fitted together, and nine cars abreast were wont to roll along it. Carriages, rare even in Europe at that time, delighted and surprised by their numbers and convenience the Western visitors.* All this glory vanished, and with changes of dynasties, decay and ruin fell on the magnificence of the great city. But it lives on; it has risen from the well-nigh complete destruction thirty years ago during the T'aip'ing Rebellion, and possibly before this century has closed, its streets may be alive again with wheeled vehicles; or, at any rate, the scream and roar of the "iron horse" and "iron way" may be heard.

Fancy is almost paralyzed when looking back over these centuries; and when imagining the lives of the generations which have passed away; their laughter and their tears; their evening and morning hours; their constant cry and aspiration, "Who will show us any good?" the storms which have gathered and burst over the land; the blue arch of the sky when the storm had passed; flood, and

* "Notes on Hangchow, Past and Present," Bishop Moule.

drought, and famine; fruitful seasons, abundant food, and gladness; and in front of them all death and the future state. How fascinating, how appalling is the retrospect! It affords, however, some slight relief to the mystery if we remember that, besides the perpetual witness to the eternal power and Godhead of the Creator uttered by the yet voiceless utterances of the heavens, and by all " things that are made," Christianity has four times entered China with the offer of mercy more or less articulately given.*

First came the Nestorians under Olopun (A.D. 635), in correspondence with Syrian Asia, as attested by the great Nestorian Tablet at Singan-fu, which itself dates from the eighth century. Olopun brought with him "The True Scriptures," "The Sacred Books," and they were translated in the Imperial Library. These churches flourished till the end of the Mongol period, about the middle of the fourteenth century. Secondly, and before the final disappearance of the Nestorian Churches, in the thirteenth century, came the Roman Church under the lead of the Franciscan Bishop, John de Monte-Corvino; and this Bishop, to his honour be it spoken, signalized his advent by the translation into Chinese of the New Testament and the Psalms. Thirdly came the Jesuits, under Matteo Ricci (1582), followed by others only second to him in eminence—Adam Schaal, Trigault, Emmanuel Diaz, men distinguished for scientific skill

* "A Brief Account of the Work of the British and Foreign Bible Society for and in China." (Canon Edmonds.)

and devotion to their work, but using science rather than Scripture as their chief weapon. Finally, all too late, arrived the Missions from Churches of the Reformation, eighty-three years ago, under Morrison; but not in any numbers or energy for a quarter of a century after that noble pioneer.

But let us take a more practical method than a mere musing retrospect, and contemplate the Chinese nation as it exists to-day; and try to pass in review the population of the land. Well, estimate the population at the lowest suggested number, 250,000,000. Let the nation march past you in single file, allowing two seconds for each individual to flash by and be gone. Let them pass on uninterruptedly and without rest day and night; and fifteen years will have run out before the solemn procession has ended. Or if you take the more probable estimate of 360,000,000, then twenty-two years will scarcely suffice, and a generation will be fast dying and dropping out of the ranks, and a new generation will be advancing through infancy and childhood, before the mighty march of the original army is over!

CHAPTER II.

A CHAPTER IN CHINESE HISTORY.
THE GREAT REBELLION: CAUSED AND ABANDONED BY CHRISTIANS.

"Unless another convulsion like the T'aip'ing Rebellion should occur (and this is by no means an impossibility), throwing over tradition bodily as did the "First Emperor" (B.C. 220), it will be a long time before China takes that place in the world to which her numbers, resources, and high civilisation justly entitle her."—*Quarterly Review*, "Western China," July, 1890.

THE glorious land which I have briefly described in my first chapter has been torn and devastated and convulsed all down the stream of time by dynastic changes, by civil war, by inroads from hostile tribes, by flood and drought, and by famine and pestilence.

The Yellow River, "China's Woe," to which I allude below, may be regarded as a native type of the nation's history. That great waterway possesses vast capacities for blessing; its very name suggests the rich deposit which it leaves all down its tortuous course. But though destined to be a fertiliser and reviver of the land, it continually bursts its bounds and runs riot over the lower level of the surrounding country. At certain long intervals it becomes extremely erratic, and finds its way to another and more ancient river-bed, leaving its more recent course dry. Then, influenced by laborious engineering works, or by some natural impetus of its own waters, it goes back again to its deserted bed; sweeping in these transits past cities which are saved sometimes with extreme difficulty from destruction by shutting fast and damming closely the massive city gates.

Similar has been the chequered course of the nation. With boundless capacities for joy or woe; with intellectual power of no mean order; with a civilisation of a comparatively advanced type; with industries and natural products leading to far-reaching commercial relations; and with a climate of wonderful variety,—yet the Chinese nation has closed chapter after chapter of its long history in blood, in desolation, and in woe.

One of these chapters I select for brief narrative, one of the most recent, and one in which we touch very closely the great subject of Christian influence and responsibility and duty. For the T'aip'ing Rebellion, which I propose briefly to describe, was in a certain sense caused and then abandoned by Christendom, and its history forms accordingly a solemn and warning lesson as to the extreme danger of failing to take advantage of opportunities.

My own personal recollections of the Rebellion as it affected Cheh-Kiang and touched Ningpo, would be too long for the limits of this small book. I confine myself chiefly to a brief history of the movement in its origin and triumphant rise and progress, till it touched Western skill and power, and withered away.

Only let me record here, with fervent thanks and praise, which the flight of years will, I trust, never chill, my remembrance of the wonderful deliverances and mercies of those days. It may encourage future missionaries in China to know how during the crisis of the Rebellion which we witnessed at Ningpo (1861-62), and during the long days of unrest and confusion which succeeded that crisis, God interfered to protect us. So wonderful was the Providence, so exactly timed the interference, that it seems in looking back to have been God's own hand visibly stretched out to save. And in our darkest hours our Lord was never out of hearing, nor His Throne of grace hard to reach. I shall never forget the deep and fresh meaning which the *Litany* conveyed to all Christian hearts, Chinese as well as English, during those days of danger and alarm. "In all time of our tribulation," and in what seemed to be "the hour of death" at hand, the good Lord delivered us.

Hung-sew-tsuen, the recognised leader of the Rebellion, was born seventy-seven years ago, in a village near Canton. The family is said to have attained to great distinction in former times, and one of the ancestors of Hung-sew-tsuen fought as generalissimo of the Mings (the last native Chinese dynasty) in their final struggle with the usurper, and the memory of this may have stimulated him in his hostility to the Manchoo Tartars. His father, though headman of his village, was only a poor husbandman; but his son, having shown marked ability, was carefully educated, and distinguished himself at the preliminary examinations. He failed, however, repeatedly at the final trial for his degree; no mark of ignorance or incompetence, indeed, when one remembers that for the degree of *siu tsai* ("accomplished talents," as the lowest of the four literary degrees is called), there are on an average 1,000 competitors at the district cities, and only 30 prizes; whilst for the second degree of *Kyü jin* ("promoted man") at the provincial capitals there may be from 10,000 to 15,000 competitors, and only 90 or 100 degrees conferred. Hung-sew-tsuen, however, would not be comforted by this reflection; and his frequent failures, attributable as he was persuaded to gross bribery and favouritism, unsettled and dissatisfied his mind. Some accounts, indeed, represent him as successful in obtaining both the first and the second degrees; but as continually barred from office by corrupt and prejudiced superiors.

In 1833 he met in Canton a strange-looking foreigner preaching; probably it was Morrison himself, for Morrison did not die till the year 1836.

Shortly after this he received from Leang-a-fah, Morrison's faithful, estimable, but poorly-educated convert, some Christian books and tracts of his own compilation. These books were laid aside for some years. In 1837 (four years later), after another failure in the examinations, he fell ill for forty days, and saw visions which were ever after quoted as the cause and the explanation of the great Rebellion. A Divine being appeared to him, so he asserted, with the command to destroy the idols and the imps— that is the Manchoos—but to spare the people. Twenty-four years later, at Ningpo, we heard the echo of those imagined voices. "Don't fear," said the T'aip'ing soldiers, as they rushed through the Ningpo streets with drawn swords; "we fight only with the imps and the idols—you people need not be alarmed." The war of 1842 opened the eyes of Hung-sew-tsuen to the power of the strange foreigners whom he had formerly seen in Canton. He bethought him of his long-neglected books, and when he began to study them he seemed to find a confirmation of his visions in their pages.

In 1844 his friend and first convert, Fung-yan-san, an earnest, simple-minded man, helped him to found in Kwangsi a "Society of Worshippers of God," giving up idolatry, and renouncing the glory and pleasures of this present evil world. These men were accustomed to meet for worship by night on the summit of lofty hills. In 1847 Hung-sew-tsuen applied for baptism to Mr. Roberts, an American Baptist Missionary at Canton, who later joined his early enquirer when he occupied Nankin. Mr. Roberts, however, deferred him, as the hope of Mission employ was obviously one motive in the application. Meanwhile the new society attracted the suspicion of the authorities, partly because of their zeal in destroying the idols; and in 1850 the little band had to stand on their defence against Imperialist soldiers sent to attack them. They were successful in their first fight, and having definitely now taken up arms, the news spread like wildfire; large crowds flocked to their standard, the standard of the Dynasty of "Great Peace"; and "every one that was in distress, and every one that was in debt, and every one that was discontented, and bitter of soul, gathered themselves together." Defence turned into attack; and in three short years they fought and burnt their way through Kwangsi, Hoonan ("Hoonan has been trodden in dust and ashes," says a contemporary Imperial decree), Hupeh, and An-hwei up to Nanking, which they stormed March 19th, 1853, and occupied for ten years as the centre of their power. Twenty thousand Manchoos were slaughtered in the sacking of this city. At this time the total T'aip'ing strength was estimated at from 60,000 to 80,000 trusted adherents, divided into five armies of 13,125 men each; besides 100,000 at least of non-combatants, doing duty as porters, trench diggers, and artificers. The whole movement was doubtless largely swollen by reinforcements from the "Triad," "White Lily," and other secret political societies. And it is worth observing that the accession of these motley crowds, most of whom were innocent of all religion, or devoted adherents of the God of War alone, may have exerted a powerful influence in neutralizing and at last obliterating the religious element in the T'aip'ings themselves.

In 1854 they advanced in two streams of war—one from Ngan-King, one from Nanking—northward till within twenty miles of T'ien-tsin, where they were checked in November by Tartar horsemen. Retiring slowly, and capturing city after city in Chili, Shantung, Shansi, and Honan, they were beleaguered in Nanking by large Imperialist forces. Here they were hard pressed, and crippled also by the terrific fights amongst the subordinate kings in Nanking, when 30,000 people were slain by violence and stratagem. The whole scene reminds one vividly of the literally suicidal conflicts within the walls during the last siege of Jerusalem. In March, 1860, the T'aip'ings broke suddenly through the cordon; and then followed the most brilliant achievements of their long campaign. They advanced rapidly on Hangchow; stormed the outer city; sacked it; and after three days of pillage and bloodshed, described to me by eye-witnesses as a time of unspeakable horror, they evacuated the city, wheeled round, passed at a distance the Imperialist host lumbering heavily in pursuit; reached Nanking; swept away the Imperialist forts and encampments; annihilated for the time the Imperialist power in that region; and 70,000 Imperialist soldiers joined the rebel force. Soochow also, with a large part of Kiangsu, fell under their sway at this time, till the great Gordon came on the scene, with his colleagues Li and Tso, of whom the first still survives as the Viceroy, Li Hung Chang. In 1861, two auxiliary armies, one apparently from Soochow and one from the S.W., moving down the Tsien-tang river, invaded the fair province of Cheh-Kiang, determined, if possible, to secure their long-felt want of a port and friendly intercourse with Western powers, which seemed impossible at Shanghai, from the hostile attitude assumed by foreigners there. They succeeded. They stormed Ningpo on December 9th, 1861, with brilliant dash and courage; and having entered into an engagement with the Consuls and

Naval Commanders of the port to respect foreigners and abstain from reckless bloodshed, they were unmolested and undisturbed during five months. But their inability to establish any firm and equitable government, their growing idleness and hostility, and the paralysis of legitimate trade, caused by their occupation of Ningpo, inevitably led to a collision. They refused Captain Roderic Dew's offer of equitable terms; they challenged him to a fight, and after a fierce encounter they were driven out on May 10th, 1862. We returned from the north bank of the river, where we had taken refuge, to our Mission home and work within the city in June; but the enraged T'aip'ings hung hovering round us for many weeks, burning and sacking Tsz-ch'i, twelve miles off, and ravaging the great Sanpo plain, thirty miles away. Gradually driven back to beyond the thirty miles radius, suddenly, on September 18th, the news startled us of the approach of a fresh force nearly 100,000 strong, through the southern passes. The city was fast shut up; the people trembled with panic and despair; the danger was imminent, as the great circuit of the city walls, five miles in length, was defended merely by small detachments of blue-jackets and marines from the British ships in the harbour. But just as the need was sorest, reinforcements from Gordon's army were sent down by Admiral Hope, who followed himself the next day. The siege was raised, and the T'aip'ings were beaten in the open field; slowly once again they were forced backwards, and Shaoushing, after desperate fighting, was captured on March 15th. They retired beyond the Tsien-tang, and held out in Hangchow for nearly twelve months. At length they abandoned the great city in the night, and the war-cloud cleared and passed away from the desolated and more than decimated province of Cheh-Kiang. The terrors of those days may be understood in part from one personal recollection of my own. I was itinerating some years later in the hills ten miles from Ningpo. It was a lovely April afternoon, and the lower slopes of the hills were red with azaleas. I pointed them out to my Chinese companion. "Ah," he said, "do you see that hill? When the T'aip'ings made their last attack on Ningpo, the people here offended them in some way; they attacked the town; all fled to the hills; and there on that hillside I saw myself dead men, women, and children lying as thick as the flowers to-day."

After their repulse in Cheh-Kiang, the T'aip'ings swept through Kiangsi into Fuh-Kien; but Nanking having fallen, and the basis of their power being overthrown, and Hung-sew-tsuen having committed suicide, the great Rebellion passed away. From first to last at least thirteen out of the eighteen provinces of China proper felt the power and the blighting influence of their presence.

"From Canton to the Great Wall," wrote the *North China Herald*, Jan. 3rd, 1857, "from the shores of the Pacific to the mountains of Thibet, there are no provinces where there have not been disorders: while in most there is now open rebellion."

Samuel Mossman, in his story, "The Mandarin's

Daughter," speaks of an area of 726,000 square miles representing 1,200 miles of latitude and 600 of longitude as traversed by the T'aip'ings, and of 10,000,000 lives as sacrificed in the struggle.

Was this, then, merely a chapter in China's long history specially stained with tears and blood; a blast of exceptional fury in the long storm of the "changes and chances" which has raged over this mortal life of ours ever since sin came in? Was it a chapter closed with no interest, save in the mere narrative, for Christian readers; a howl and shriek of the wind which came and went, and which we hear no more?

CHAPTER III.

THE GREAT REBELLION—THE STORM GOING DOWN.

COMPARATIVELY little, from personal observation, is known of the religious character of the T'aip'ing Rebellion during the years which elapsed between their first taking up arms and their contact with foreigners at Nanking, at Soochow, and at Ningpo. Probably the very fact of taking up arms, professedly for the violent and compulsory propagation of the religion of Him who died a violent death voluntarily to save men from ruin, gradually blighted, as in such cases generally takes place, and soon well-nigh destroyed the early Christian element. I do not touch here upon the question of the lawfulness of rebellion and revolution. It was the mixture of the two movements—religious reform and political revolt against magisterial oppression—which probably ruined the enterprise. "They are robbers and Christians; they are Christians and robbers," said an irate Chinaman to Sir G. Bonham in 1853.

And yet one cannot refuse to recognise the conspicuous courage (I had almost written faith) of the T'aip'ing leaders in daring to link on to a popular political movement the profession of the religion of the unpopular foreigner. This was felt at certain stages of the movement very strongly;

and in 1854 a body of 2,000 men from the south, coming to join the T'aip'ings, went over to the Imperialists rather than become compulsory Christians. It is a phenomenon worthy of prolonged study, that an able and powerful man, setting up a Chinese dynasty in opposition to the alien family then reigning, and supported by a large fighting army, should think it good policy, and likely to serve his lofty aspirations, to proclaim as *his* creed the religion of that alien Western nation which had, even during the very progress of the Rebellion, so weakened and humiliated his country by disastrous and, as many think, dishonourable wars. I cannot expound the phenomenon; but it holds out the hope that when accompanied "not by might, nor by power, but by the Spirit of the Lord of Hosts," Christian truth is proclaimed throughout China's wide provinces, the Gospel will spread with swift conquering power, and the hold of the people on their old faiths will be as easily loosened as it was in these terrible T'aip'ing days.

Another circumstance should lead us to yield just meed of praise to the T'aip'ings. They earnestly desired the friendship of foreigners; yet in one thing, at least would they agree with the hated Manchoos whom they were extirpating—namely, in the avowed intention to annihilate the trade in opium, so dear in those days to foreigners.

In its earliest stage this remarkable movement was, so far as religion is concerned, Protestant in Christian doctrine, worshipping one God, waging war against image worship, and observing Sunday; and opium smoking and spirit drinking were ranged under infractions of the Seventh Commandment. Abundant reasons are hinted at in these tenets and principles for the malignant hatred with which the movement was regarded by many critics both ecclesiastical and mercantile. But the comparative apathy with which the Protestant Churches of Christendom viewed the movement is not so easy of explanation. There was a proposal set on foot, and partially carried out in 1857-8 to raise funds for the printing and distribution of 1,000,000 New Testaments in China, agitated and convulsed by a semi-Christian movement. But when the earthquake of the Rebellion was over, conspicuous amongst the ruins were to be seen, as I saw with my own eyes, "the idols utterly abolished" by Chinese hands. The temples were burnt and thrown down, and not a whole image was to be seen in city or country for hundreds of miles, save where by secret heavy bribes some special temple had been spared. No tongue was raised any more in defence of idolatry and in praise of idols ; and it was admitted with a sad smile of perplexity and despair that gods which could not keep their own heads on their shoulders could not well be expected to preserve their worshippers from murder and rapine. The poor people delivered from the terrible incubus of the T'aip'ing inroad, and the equal horrors of an Imperialist rally, recognised with warm gratitude their deliverers in Christian England and France and America ; and with their old beliefs thus shattered and disgraced, they were ready to listen to the missionary's voice telling of a better hope, and of an

Almighty Saviour and Deliverer. Why, then, I ask, and no answer has yet reached me, why was this supreme opportunity let slip by the Church at home? It *was* thus let slip! The Churches in America were paralysed by their own momentous life-and-death struggle; but in England there was no sufficient reason for the melancholy and well-nigh appalling fact that between 1862 and 1864—*the* golden days for occupying the land for our Lord—*no* reinforcement from the Church of England, and scarcely any from other Christian bodies reached the waiting land.

Soon, too soon, idolatry raised its head, and reappeared from the ashes; temples were rebuilt, and idols set on their pedestals again and repainted. *That* opportunity passed by, and in such a form will probably never return; for now that missionaries are, thank God, pouring into the land, as they *should* have poured in thirty years ago, they find idolatry rehabilitated and strong.

I have dwelt thus far chiefly on the effects of the T'aip'ing Rebellion; but what shall we say to the movement itself? What would have been the state of China now, were she ruled by a Christian dynasty, and by statesmen heartily friendly with Christian Powers? What might have followed, we cannot but exclaim, had the strange movement possessed wiser guides and counsellors; had they *kept* the rule laid down in the Proclamation of 1851 never to go into the villages to seize people's goods; had the Bible been introduced as the text-book in the Public Service Examinations, bringing with it the study of the Book in its original languages, as T. T. Meadows anticipated in 1857; had the distinct elevation in the status of woman which, for a time, was observed in Nanking, spread through the land; and had the lust of rapine and the intoxication of success been restrained? The arrival of Hung-jin, cousin of Hung-sew-tsuen, and formerly an evangelist at Hong-Kong in Mission employ, exercised in 1860 a favourable effect for a while, both at Soochow and in Nanking. One clause in Hung-jin's proclamation, issued by him as the Kan Wang, or "Shield King" of the Dynasty, runs in hopeful lines: "Foreigners are never to be called by opprobrious names. Missionaries are to travel and to live and to preach everywhere. Railroads and steamboats, fire and life insurance companies, and newspapers, are to be freely introduced for the good of China." Street-preaching was allowed and was carried on in 1860 round the palace of the "Heavenly King" in Nanking, and amidst crowds of the Chang-maou, or "Long-Haired," as the rebels were called, from the fact of their abandoning the long queue and allowing their hair to fall unplaited and unkempt.

Much hope was entertained by some of those who visited Soochow and even Nanking, of ultimate good out of abounding evil. But the evil for the time triumphed. The Shield King himself could not resist the force of the tide, and in his latter days he was guilty of gross cruelty and violence. The opinion of a sober and at first favourably prejudiced observer, the late Bishop Russell, was that the rebels at Ningpo had no religion, were worse than the heathen, and lacked well-nigh wholly those two bright features in Chinese character, education and politeness.

A few brief reflections on the history and character of the movement will fitly close this narrative of the T'aip'ing Rebellion. (1) The retrospect, even at a distance of thirty years, is sufficient to make one shudder at the extreme horror of civil strife. The T'aip'ings advancing in triumph, massacred ruthlessly the people who made the slightest show of resistance, or who refused to abandon the tail and the tonsure. The Imperialists rallied and drove back the T'aip'ings, and they too in the line of their victorious march massacred savagely all found with unshaven heads, or who were known to have submitted, however unwillingly, to the T'aip'ings. No wonder that in these awful days of dilemma suicide abounded. I have seen myself many ponds in San-po which had been filled not long before with the bodies of women who had flung themselves in as the only hope of escape. In Hangchow from 50,000 to 70,000 are said to have perished in one week, and a large number of these from suicide. God in His mercy ward off from China the repetition of such scenes of horror!

(2) It is possible that this narrative may throw much light upon the ill-disguised opposition to Christianity manifested so often by Chinese officials and by the literary class generally. In the year 1858, San-ko-lin-sin, the Imperialist Cavalry leader, and in 1860 the Governor of Kiang-si, memorialised the Throne against Christianity, and stigmatised it as revolutionary and in league with the rebels. This is hardly to be wondered at since the gigantic T'aip'ing

movement began under a Christian profession, and Chinese soldiers and civilians could hardly be expected to understand how, even under a political régime the most galling and oppressive, Christianity has been emphatically loyal to the powers that be. "Custom to whom custom is due; fear to whom fear; honour to whom honour. Fear God; honour the king."

"Christianity," says Mozley, "gave room for national feeling, for patriotism, for that common bond which a common history creates; for loyalty, for pride in the grandeur of the nation's traditions, for joy in success." Yet it can afford to abjure all carnal weapons in its conquering march. "In its own world war would be impossible; but it is no part of the mission of Christianity to reconstruct the order of the world."

This is abundantly true, but the Chinese did not know it, and so one could not but welcome the roar of English guns on May 10th, 1862, that first stroke of the death-knell of the Rebellion. It afforded a complete answer to the sneer, "You Christians are in league with our oppressors, the destroyers of our dynasty, and with no reconstructive power of their own." "Strange, if so," we replied, "that Christian powers should have driven out their brethren and allies by force of arms."

(3) But some of my readers may be disposed to ask why England and France took sides at all in China's internecine struggle, and whether the expulsion of the T'aip'ings from Ningpo and their chastisement round Shanghai can be justified by any principles of international morality.

There was every inducement on the side of England to help the T'aip'ings. The Imperial Government had been guilty of distinct treachery in 1859, causing thereby the repulse at the Taku forts. But England had secured a treaty of amity with the ruling dynasty, and she declined to be swayed by feelings of revenge into an unworthy infringement of this treaty, in effect if not in form, by aiding the would-be destroyers of the dynasty.

Wherever it was possible, as for instance in the first capture of Ningpo by the T'aip'ings, England stood aside and permitted fair play. But when her own treaty rights of trade and peaceable residence were invalidated, and the lives and property of her subjects on Chinese soil were imperilled, what else could England do than interpose in assertion of her legal rights and privileges?

I have discussed these points thus briefly in order to meet by anticipation objections which may rise in the minds of my readers. Two truths at any rate arise and shine upon us as we close the narrative: "Not by might, nor by power, but by the Spirit of the Lord" alone is His kingdom set up on earth. But it is the great duty of the Church of Christ to be ever on guard and on the watch to enter in and possess in her Master's Name lands thrown open for the Gospel by the conflicts and revolutions of nations.

CHAPTER IV.

THE GREAT REBELLION—AFTERMATH OF THE HARVEST OF WOE.

ONE of the most remarkable after-influences of the T'aip'ing rebellion was the long succession of rumours which summer after summer have agitated the people in Cheh-Kiang, and in other far-off regions of the empire.

These rumours will probably diminish rapidly in number and intensity so soon as railways traverse the land. A great main line from Hankow to T'ien-tsin had already been surveyed, and sanctioned by Government; and the able and energetic Viceroy of Canton had been transferred to Hankow expressly with the object of pushing forward this great work. Suddenly the commencement of the railway was countermanded, apparently with the intention of executing the whole by native capital, skill, and steel. The delay, however, is in all probability only temporary; and but a natural pause before the initiation of an enterprise which will produce a real though peaceable revolution in the land.

The establishment of newspapers and of the telegraph has already done much to dissipate the clouds and mists of misconception and superstition.

But in past times these rumours have done much to hinder and to blight evangelistic work; and the danger has not yet passed away. The narratives which follow will not, therefore, be without interest in connection with Mission work in China.

The natural history of some of these rumours is a study well worthy of attention. Supposing, as was the fact in the cases I am about to mention, that there is no foundation at all for the rumour, how is it first set going? who first invents it, and why? How came this lying inventor to collect a credulous audience, and to speak so persuasively as to set the ball of nonsense rolling, till, as in North and Mid China, the rumour, growing and expanding in its course, traversed and agitated and convulsed vast stretches of country? And what accounts for the sudden silence which often falls on the mischievous clamouring tongues? The most plausible explanation is, that these stories are the work of secret insurrectionary societies with which indeed in many parts of China society is literally honeycombed. The minds of the people are excited by these stories, and are prepared for any startling surprise. Then, if in addition to alarm and unrest, foreigners can be involved in suspicion on account of these magical arts, and onslaughts can be followed by hostilities between the Imperialist forces and these foreign powers, the supreme opportunity for insurrection will have arrived. All these symptoms occurred in the series of rumours which disturbed China during the summer and autumn of 1877;

and at that time war was imminent, in consequence of the treacherous murder of Mr. Margary. It was a strange but significant coincidence that Ningpo was agitated by precisely the same rumours more than thirty years before, about the time, that is, of her capture by the British forces in the course of the second great war between England and China.

One rumour was to the effect that persons were crushed and suffocated when in bed by paper-men which were sent aloft by magical influence, and descended gradually, increasing in size, and changing into different forms, now appearing as a weighty black cat, now as a yet heavier and more oppressive buffalo. At Su-chow, in the province of Kiangsu, one of the first victims is said to have been a woman, who struggled violently against the supernatural oppression, and springing out of bed, discovered on the floor a paper-man. She fastened it to the room door; and the next day a Buddhist priest appeared, asking for money. The woman refused to help him. "Well, if you have no money, give me the paper figure on your door upstairs," he said. She went upstairs, tore it off the door, cut it to pieces with scissors, and brought it down to the priest; but the priest was dead. This story set the place on fire; and the people were so convulsed by combined terror and anger that, when the rumour swept into Hangchow, two men were seized on suspicion of magical arts in a market-town near the great city, and were burnt alive in the market-place. I passed through that busy town two months later; and even then the agitation of the people was a most alarming phenomenon.

The wave of rumour and excitement swept down from the north-west, and crossing the river Yangtsze, touched Huchow on the great Lake; it shook and convulsed Soochow; and with no little anxiety did we in Hangchow await the approach of this mysterious visitation. At length, on Saturday afternoon, September 10th, 1877, we heard that the wave had entered the great northern suburb of the city, about five miles from my house; and at 10.30 p.m., on Sunday, November 11th, as if by a bound, it appeared close to my own door. It had been a day of specially laborious duty; and tired with the day's work, I was pacing to and fro in my verandah, when I heard first of all a strange suppressed cry, as of one suffocated and struggling to be free, in the lane outside my garden wall; then followed an unearthly scream, with a sound as of horses trampling on a boarded floor; then the sounding of gongs, and loud shouts, and running to and fro. "It has come," we exclaimed. "The danger, if danger there be, has found its way to our very doors." It seemed the wisest plan to brave the risk of suspicion, and to go boldly out and see if we could help the people in their terror. So, carefully unbarring our gate, I sallied forth with my Chinese servant, and elbowing my way through the crowd, I asked what was the matter. "Oh! he has *come*," they replied in manifest terror. "*Who* has come?" I asked again. "The man, of course—the paperman. He has come and gone." "Well," I replied, "never mind the paper-man, for I have my doubts about him; but where is the man on to whom you say he, the paper-man, fell?"

They led me at once into a silk weaver's house; and there, in the middle of the room, panting for breath and gesticulating, stood a young man. He told me that he had been in bed only a few minutes when the curtains were thrown aside, and a heavy weight seemed to fall on him. I asked him what he had eaten for supper; I told him that as his pulse was high, and his skin feverish, I thought it proceeded from nightmare, caused by a heavy meal, and following on a day and long evening spent in talking about these rumours. "At any rate," I said, "what *can* be the use of gongs and shouting? In any fear or anxiety cast all your care on the great God of heaven. In the words of your own proverbial language—

"'Great Heaven adore, so far, so near;
High glancing gaze, low stooping ear.'"

He thanked me, and went to bed again; and I too retired, but not to rest; for all through that sultry night, again and again, we heard from the neighbouring houses the same unearthly scream, as one after another was smitten by the curious delusion.

At the same time, but a little earlier in the summer, the tail-cutting rumour agitated Hangchow and large districts of Central China. This strange and in some senses inexplicable phenomenon was more obviously connected with political intrigue than the paper-man rumour described above. The tail, or long plaited queue of the Chinese, is, in a sense, a badge of conquest, having been imposed upon the conquered race by the Manchoos; and the clipping off of the tails would be taken by the people as an intimation from secret political societies that the day of their deliverance from the Manchoo rule was at hand. The story was that, without a twitch or jerk, or any sound of shears or scissors cutting through the thick plaits of the queue, it would be severed and fall by some unseen agency; and terror was added to the magic by the rumour that the man who lost his tail would die within three days at the nearest, or within 300 days at the furthest limit. Two persons in connection with our own Mission in Hangchow lost parts of their queues without any apparent cause. In the one case a catechist was kneeling in his cottage at prayers; and when he rose from his knees, greatly to his astonishment and the dismay of his family, two-thirds of his tail lay on the floor. We suspected a schoolboy who was in the cottage at the time of having mischievously severed his teacher's tail. But if he was guilty of this freak, sudden vengeance fell upon him. The next day he called at my house, and returned at once to his father's cottage. It was a brilliant afternoon in midsummer; he saw no one in the three hundred yards which led to his home; he felt no check or touch; but when he entered his father's door to his amazement *his* tail also was gone. Both man and boy appeared in church the next day, and the whole congregation was perplexed by these strange occurrences; but I trust we all found rest and peace in the love and wisdom of Him whose hand controls and brings to confusion the devices and magic of men. During many days in Hangchow, especially when the rumour began to gain credence that the foreign missionaries were in league with the plotters and the magicians, men would tightly grasp the end of their tails held over the shoulder, or wind them securely round their heads, and sidle across the streets so as to avoid our touch. Meanwhile Buddhist and Taoist priests improved the opportunity by the sale of special charms, and by the arrangement of long processions with

CHINAMAN WITH QUEUE WOUND ROUND THE HEAD.

gongs and lanterns all the night through, and till the sun was actually up, for which they expected liberal fees and donations to their temples. The sound of the gong was supposed to alarm and put to flight the workers of these magical arts. Upon which, in Su-chow, every gong was sold; and in Hangchow the price for a small hand-gong rose from two shillings to fourteen. Umbrellas also

were opened indoors as well as in the open air to
intercept these falling paper-men ; and the umbrella
shops were speedily well-nigh emptied of their whole
stock-in-trade. A week's darkness—darkness that
could be felt — was prophesied to commence on
September 18th, 1876 (the sun, however, on that
day shone with unclouded splendour). Insurrection
was to break out on September 25th, 1876 (but the
day closed in peace). Meanwhile the students for
the great triennial examinations, 10,000 and more
in number, were crowding into the city from the
whole of the agitated province. They came up full
of the rumours and of the consequent panic with
which their country homes had been shaken. At
all times ready for mischief, and causing anxiety to
the mandarins during their stay in the great city,
they came now fired with animosity against the few
missionaries (the only foreigners) residing in the
city. It was a time of grave alarm and serious
danger; and very special prayer was offered up for
God's gracious help and the interposition of the
might of His arm. Suddenly and unexpectedly the
answer came. The high mandarins, alarmed at
the agitation in the country, issued simultaneously
four proclamations, signed and sealed by the Viceroy
of Nanking, by the Governor of Cheh-Kiang, and by
the Prefects of Su-chow and Hangchow, commanding
the people to " be quiet, and do every man his own
business ; attempting nothing rashly." The rumours
were denounced as foolish imaginations. The crime
of their circulation and of magical arts, if they
existed at all, was laid to the charge of the " White
Lotus " political society, one of the numerous illegal

combinations amongst the Chinese. The beating of gongs was prohibited, and it was expressly stated that the whole affair was "totally unconnected with the European sects of the Lord of Heaven (Roman Catholic) and of the Holy Religion of Jesus (other Christians)." Thus spoke the Governor of Cheh-Kiang; and the Viceroy of Nanking, with no preconceived prejudice in favour of Christians, but rather the reverse, added in his official utterance the assurance that Christian Chinese were as orderly and law-abiding as any under his jurisdiction.

Where were these proclamations posted? Conspicuously on the great gates leading to the vast examination enclosure at Hangchow, with its broad central street; and its lanes running at right angles on either side; a hundred sentry boxes or cells in each lane, with a seat and a table-board in front; the whole giving accommodation for 10,000 at least. Through these gates the long stream of students must of necessity pass on their way to their weary session of three days and three nights, thrice repeated, in those close cells during the most unhealthy season of the year; and as they passed, they read, to their astonishment and chagrin, the complete vindication of the honour and integrity of those foreigners, and of that religion which they had denounced and longed to exterminate.

So in very truth did God "make the wrath of man to praise Him, and the residue of wrath He restrained."

It must be remembered that in addition to the distraction of mind and positive danger caused by these spasmodic outbursts of superstitious folly, Missions in China have to contend with a *chronic* state of superstition ; an atmosphere from the folds of which it is hard wholly to lift the minds even of sincere converts. The foolish story, which not long ago prevailed from Pekin to Canton, and frightened into unbelief and hostility countless hopeful inquirers, was to the effect that at the death of converts the foreign missionary insisted on being present in order to remove the eyes and liver of the departed, which, by a refinement of ironical folly, were traced to Western lands, compounded with opium, and sent back to bewitch and poison the living. I have heard and seen myself over and over again the fatal effects of this story (possibly an extravagant guess at the accompaniments of extreme unction); but it seems scarcely conceivable that an intelligent people like the Chinese should be thus swayed by insensate folly. Another powerful engine in the great adversary's hands for the hindrance of interest and inquiry is supplied by the prevalent belief in witchcraft ; and oftentimes after a Christian's sun has set in peace, leaving a bright afterglow of example and consistent conversation, a witch has been hired by some opponent of Christianity. She pretends to call up the departed saint, and to ascertain from the spirit how he fares in the unseen world. With groans and laments in the mouth of this lying agent, the dead Christian is made to bewail his folly, for he can obtain no admission into the ancestral temple by front or backdoor ; and misled by this lie, relatives and friends turn back and walk no more with us.

CHAPTER V.

FLOOD AND FAMINE.

Since the great earthquake of the T'aiping Rebellion China has suffered repeatedly from drought and famine, and these appalling calamities have affected not remotely the work of evangelization. In some quarters the frequent repetition of appeals for charitable help from Western lands creates the impression of the unreality of the suffering, as if China were in a chronic state of flood. It must be remembered, however, how vast the area of the Empire is, and the peculiar arrangement of its water-ways. Even local and occasional disasters of this kind affect great multitudes of people. The sudden rush of water down the slopes of the Dorset hills, near Cerne, last summer, whether caused by water-spout or thunder-shower, endangered the lives of only a few school-children out for their picnic. In China, many villages would have been overwhelmed. The bursting of the great reservoir at Johnstown, in America, was an appalling disaster indeed, but in China, with her dense population, and fewer appliances for relief and rescue, the terror and the destruction would have been tenfold greater.

The Yellow River, "China's Woe," as it is called, though able, with right direction and control, to be

China's blessing, is never to be trusted. Freshets, caused by the melting of the snows in the mountains, and by the summer rains, break down again and again embankments raised by the patient and persistent toil of the Chinese, and inundate vast stretches of the low-lying country on either side. A series of artificial lakes, in addition to the natural lakes along its course, is suggested by engineers as necessary to hold and retain the overflow, and prevent its devastating march over the land.

Terrific must be the scenes accompanying some of these floods. I witnessed, on a very small scale, the *possibilities* of flood in China a year ago, when spending a short time during the extreme heat of summer on the hills near Ningpo.

The Chinese believe that the dragon is the "Rain King," and to the sceptical on this point they would say, "Observe his tail." And there, sure enough, when a water-spout hangs over the sea, or more rarely moves over the land, let down from the bulging cloud above, sucking up and lashing in mad sport the water below, or breaking loose and rushing in havoc across the fields, you see the dragon's tail. The Dragon King's lineage is thus traced :—A toad resides in a hill, and expands there in size and wisdom. At certain special seasons, great torrents of rain fall to commemorate and signalize the coming event. The hill-sides slip in long lines of stone and sand; the toad escapes, and passes out to sea on the flood to compete in "the examination for the degree of dragon;" so literary are the Chinese, even in their most foolish superstitions. The name for landslip at Ningpo is "the escape of the frog," or "the escape of the dragon." This outward sign of the mysterious Rain King's evolution was conspicuous in the course of the flood which I describe below, for the bursting springs and rushing avalanches of stone and sand furrowed the hills on every side. The weather was perfect for Chinese summer days during the first three weeks of August. The cuckoo was still in full song during the morning and evening hours. (I have heard it sing indeed as late as August 21st, after which it flies southwards, and winters in the island of Formosa.) And though the flowers had nearly vanished under the extreme heat, the green of the hills, covered as they were with brushwood, with dwarf-oak, and fir-woods, and groves and forests of feathery waving bamboo, refreshed and rested the eye weary with the hot glare of the cities. One afternoon we reached, after a hot long climb, the last slope of the fine Sih-san, or Pewter Hill, 2,000 feet above the sea. From the point where we rested we could see afar many of the stations on the Ningpo Mission field. There lay the great city itself, with 400,000 souls; a brown blotch on the shining landscape, and out of the brown mass rose, like a dark pencil, the pagoda, 140 feet high. The reaches of the river inland and seawards wound like silver threads, and below the city like a broad silver ribbon. There lay the town of Tsz-chi, or "Mercy Stream," nestling amongst the northern hills. There ran the sea-line, with the gleam of the sea and the outline of the Chusan archipelago beyond. There slept in the sunshine the Loh-do-gyiao region, where not a few souls, as I describe below, have been turned from darkness to light, and from the power of Satan to God. Face southwards, and the lake shines like a shield where the hills, which encompass it, slope and dip in their undulations. Dzang-kò lies there in the centre of the plain. Tsông-ts'eng, Da-le, Gao-san, Zah-ling (names, however grotesque to the English reader, full of the hopes and sorrows of evangelization to the Ningpo workers) are all in sight from the summit of Sih-san, and beyond the northern hills we can imagine Kwun-hae-we and Ming-ngoh-dziang.

A sudden squall prevented our reaching the actual summit; so we started homewards along the narrow ridge of the great spur of Sih-san, which after a three miles' stride reaches the Ningpo plain near O-Kô.

The plain looked beautiful and luxuriantly fertile in the evening light. The second crop of rice was beginning to ripen; and was gilded now by the beams of the setting sun. Presently, on the banks of the mountain stream in the higher valley, we were enchanted at finding whole sheets of the "bridegroom flower," scarlet and white.

Three days passed; and the whole of this rich plain, thirty miles long and twenty wide, stood four feet deep in water. The hills, so peaceful that afternoon, were torn and scarred in a hundred places by landslips; and the beautiful bowery course of the mountain stream, which had been bordered with flowers, was unrecognizable amidst the mass of great boulder stones and sand and trees prostrate and barked white by the rushing torrent. The catastrophe came on slowly. First some early showers on the morning after our walk; showers with bright intervals between. Then steady and continuous rain, which after some hours swelled a little the mountain streams. Then a quiet half-day of overcast and ominous skies. Then wind and thunder and sheets of rain; and so portentous a gloom at mid-day, so dense a darkness, that our messenger from Ningpo having reached the hillside with extreme difficulty from the flooded plain, dared not move, but cowered under a rock the whole afternoon and following night, as he could not see his way. Amidst this gloom, and above the roar of wind and thunder, we heard from time to time a crashing sound, which we thought to be only some louder thunder-clap, but which was in reality the rush of the avalanches of stones close to us. Suddenly the deeply-cut watercourses on either side of the house lost all control over the streams, which now fell like a cataract upon us, and began to undermine the outer walls. Part of the wall fell inwards, and we were obliged hastily to abandon that wing of the house. Saturday evening closed upon us in gloom. We could not but feel gravely anxious at the very near and great danger. Another six hours' heavy rain would probably have caused the entire collapse of our dwelling, and the sweeping of its ruins into the valley below. I thought at one time, when the danger seemed nearest, that we might be obliged to escape higher up the hill, finding our way as best we could through the storm and darkness to a shed erected over a Buddhist priest's tomb. I had often sat there with our children on spring and summer days, enjoying the view of the great plain and the mountains beyond. I thought that we might manage to cower under this poor shed till daybreak. The very proposal seemed, however, to add to the terror of our situation, and to our children's alarm. It was well that, through God's mercy, we did not attempt the walk; for between us and that tomb an avalanche of earth and sand and trees and huge boulder stones had fallen right across the pathway; and if it had not overwhelmed us, it would at any rate have completely blocked the passage. At eight o'clock, through God's mercy, the rain abated; and at midnight the perpetual dropping from the eaves had ceased. A keen northerly breeze sprang up, and as we watched through the night, the air, for August, felt bitterly cold. I woke early on Sunday morning and mounted the hill at the back; and turning my gaze towards the plain, it looked like the open sea; one great expanse of water stretching from the foot of the hills on which I stood to the southern hills twenty miles distant; the taller trees alone traced some of the waterways, and the situation of the towns and hamlets. There was no sign of life for some hours. Then at last we saw a few boats moving about in deep water, where fields and paths and bridges should have been seen. As the day advanced, and the water began slowly to subside, partly under the blast of the northerly wind, partly by the gradual current setting seawards, we saw a green gleam spread over the floods. It was the luxuriant rice-plants which had been wholly submerged, and were now slowly reappearing as the waters fell.

It was impossible for three days to procure boats to escape from our precarious situation and reach Ningpo. Had we started a few hours earlier our route would have been over instead of under many of the bridges. Along the twelve miles of canal we saw again and again the water like a mill-race rushing into the poor people's shops and houses. Yet, though up to their knees in water, and everything soaked and spoiled by the damp, they were plying their trades with patience and sometimes with merry laughter. There was no loss of life in the plain, but amongst the hills the sudden outburst of the flood caused many deaths. In one beautiful upland village, " Under Stream," as it is called, seventy were drowned out of a total population of only 120. The village lay near the head of a narrow valley, above and by the side of which wound the course of the mountain stream. Secure even amidst the roar of the waters after the great thunderstorms of a hundred summers, the village was not alarmed till, like a Niagara wall, the mass of the flood poured down upon them. The people clambered on to the roofs of their houses, or climbed in haste the trees near; but seventy corpses lay along the valley the next day. Whole families were drowned together; amongst them the relatives of some of our Christian converts.

Two of the survivors of that awful catastrophe have been baptised during the present year; and we cannot but hope that God will bring mercy from this great judgment. Far into the hills every bridge was carried away and hurled down the roaring stream. On many of those bridges I have preached in past years, and I remember well the shrines filled with guardian deities which in many cases crowned them. All went down before the flood. The "images," things which, as the Hebrew word implies, "may be rolled about as senseless logs or lumps,"* were trundled down the stream. Our Mission chapel at Gaosan was partly carried away; but the inner room, with the Lord's Table, was unhurt.

No such flood had occurred in those beautiful hills within the memory of man. Yet this was but a small local catastrophe, and in no sense comparable with the tremendous devastations of the Yellow River.

Famine is the sure accompaniment of these greater devastations; for in those cases the food supply is swept away, and the seed for next year's sowing as well; whilst the ground is in many regions rendered unfit for cultivation by the drift and silt of stones and sand. And famine was within a few days march of us in Kiangsu and Cheh-Kiang, shortly after the flood which I have described above. The later rice was half-ruined by continuous rain, and the poor people actually went about the fields in boats tying the heavy sodden rice-ears to high sticks, so as to lift them out of the water and give them a chance of drying. In this way by patient and persistent toil, about three parts in ten of the rice and cotton were saved. Another week of rain, however, would have

* See in Jeremiah l. 2, Cambridge Bible for Schools.

ruined the whole; and prices were rapidly rising to famine rates when a northerly gale sprang up, and clear weather, through God's mercy, set in.

One effect of these great calamities is to lead some people to regard famine relief, and philanthropic alleviation of suffering, as *the* one great outlet for Christian charity towards China; to the obscuration, for the time at any rate, of the yet greater and more imperative charity of "*saving souls alive.*"

On the other hand the generous and ready response to China's appeals for temporal relief has produced from time to time a profound impression both on the rulers and people. In the words of one of our Consuls during the great famine of 1877, " the heroic courage of the almoners of the charity of Christendom amongst the famine-stricken Chinese has done more to break down the walls of prejudice and opposition than years of diplomacy could have done."

And as a consequence of this a prejudice in favour of the religion of these philanthropic foreigners has been in a measure created.

Surely the brief sketch which I have given of one of the least of "China's woes" may sound like a trumpet call to us, urging us to send to the Chinese the message of salvation before a greater flood comes " and takes them all away."

CHAPTER VI.

RELIGIOUS THOUGHT AND PRACTICE IN CHINA.

THE singular and perhaps unique phenomenon meets us in the study of Chinese religious thought and profession, that the same individual will himself believe and practice, or approve of the practice in his family, of all the three great religions in the land, Confucianism, Buddhism, and Taoism.

In a curious tract, entitled "A Guide to True Vacuity," written evidently by a Taoist, whilst "the way" (Taoism) is praised, and its cultivation inculcated, the true decorum of "the school" (Confucianism) is held up as all essential; and at the same time the recitation of Buddha's name is strongly recommended. "The canonical books of the three religions," says this anonymous writer, " are truly mysterious."*

And the spectacle is often to be seen of a rich man's funeral being conducted by a posse of Buddhist and Taoist priests, with their differing vestments and ritual; the departed having been without doubt a Confucianist.

Does not this phenomenon emphasize the necessity

* See Journal of the China Branch of the Royal Asiatic Society, vol. xxiii., 1888. Article by Bishop Moule.

and the solemn duty laid on each one of us of telling or sending *at once* to these poor dreamers as to the Way, the Truth, and the Life, the knowledge of Him who in Himself gives them the great three-fold Reality?

I proceed to give a brief account of each of these religions.

I.—CONFUCIANISM.

> "Of heaven and hell I have no power to sing;
> I cannot ease the burden of your fears;
> Nor make quick-coming death a little thing;
> Nor bring again the pleasures of past years."
>   *The Earthly Paradise.*

"The word of the truth of the Gospel."—*Col.* i. 5.

An orderly and systematic digest of Confucian teaching is beyond the scope of these brief chapters. Literature, whose first germs lie certainly 3,000 years back, would have to be described and quoted for such a purpose.*

I can offer merely a sketch of some of the leading features of this great system. It is difficult to call it a religion; and yet it is the only thing like a respectable and authorised religion in China. Religion it is not, for it may be regarded as a supreme effort at being "good without God, and moral without a religion." Yet so inextricably is the bent of the human mind "bound up" with the idea of God, that Confucius himself is worshipped; and the worship of ancestors, which Confucius found fully established before his day, and which he confirmed and

---

* Dr. Faber's "Systematic Digest of Confucian Doctrine," page 28.

blessed, satisfies in ordinary Chinese minds some of the cravings of this religious tendency. The dead are not merely canonized; they are deified, as the powerful instruments in some far-off Supreme Hand for good or for evil; for the Supreme Being is regarded as out of hearing and out of reach for ordinary mortals. The dead are supposed to be aware of what goes on in the world, and to reward or punish in accordance with the reverence and dutiful care accorded to their shades by the survivors.

> " There must be wisdom with great death.
> The dead shall look me through and through."*

Love and fear, the two mightiest motors in the human heart, join forces therefore in this religious observance : love, not seldom true love, for the dead ; and fear, for the most part omnipotent fear, of the vengeance of the unseen spirits. And when to these you add superstitious additions to these old customs; as, for instance, the idea that the departed soul depends for subsistence on the food offerings of the living, and that any interruption in the line entails loss and discomfort on the generations past, it is not difficult to estimate the force of this system. I remember well a sudden, and at first inexplicable, cessation in an old woman's inquiry after the truth. She had welcomed us with eager interest on many succeeding visits. She had apparently received the truth in the love of it ; when suddenly she was "not at home" when I called. I was so certain that she *was* at home, that I waited patiently but persistently

* Tennyson.

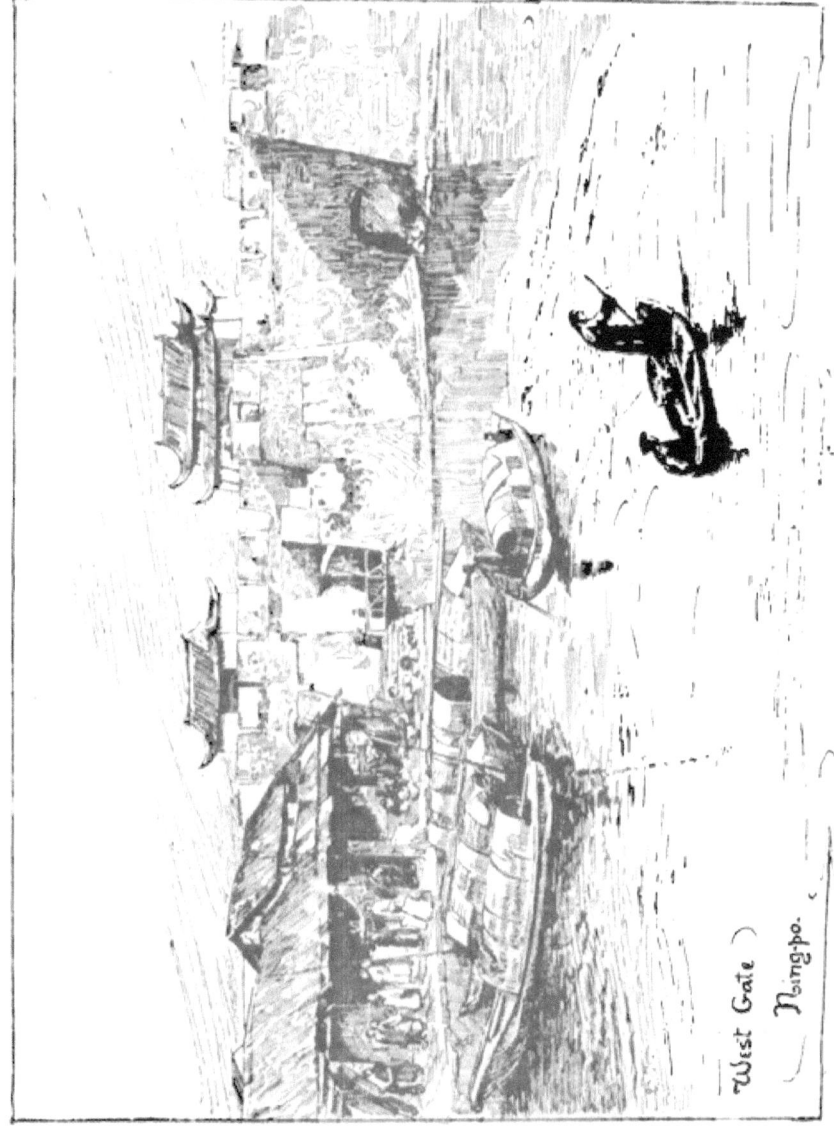
West Gate Ningpo.

till, with much hesitation and many protestations, the old woman was brought in to see me. "What is the matter?" I asked. "Nothing," she replied. "Nothing! Was all your interest in the love of the Lord Jesus nothing, then? Will you abandon your hope of heaven for nothing?" "I will tell you what is the matter," interposed a bystander. "Our old mother has been told that if she becomes a Christian her son will not worship her spirit, or make offerings at her tomb: and she does not like the prospect of being starved." Doubtless this was a somewhat gross and outspoken instance; but doubtless, also, such fears underlie, though inarticulately, the thoughts about the future world in most Chinese minds.

Yet when these hopes and fears are analysed they are found not to be essentially Confucian at all. The lines which I quote above, from Morris' *Earthly Paradise*, describe with singular and mournful accuracy the negations of Confucianism.

"*Of heaven and earth I have no power to sing.*"

"I know little enough about this life," said Confucius, in answer to eager questions from his disciples; "how can I tell you what comes after death?" "*No power to sing!*" No note: no whisper even about this eternal world, of which, nevertheless, the Chinese mind dreams and speculates!

"*I cannot ease the burden of your fears.*"

That spectral terror which rises whenever conscience awakes—the fear of retribution in the future; the expectation of a good place of beatitude for the good, and of an evil place for the wicked; and the suspicion that their common proverb may prove true: "There are but two good people: one dead; one not born." No cure for their burdening fears could Confucius suggest, for he thought that if you sin against Heaven there is no place for prayer ("Analects" iii. 13 (23).

"*Nor make quick-coming death a little thing.*"

The narrative of the death of "the Master," Confucius himself, which bears authenticity on the face of its brief ancient story, is well calculated to make "quick-coming death" a terror indeed, or at best, a prospect of calm despair. In the year B.C. 478, early one morning, very shortly before his death, he got up from his couch, and with his hands behind his back, dragging his staff, he moved about his door, repeating the sad words:

"The great mountain must crumble;
And the wise man withers away like a plant."

Confucius does not ridicule death. He does not minimise its solemnity. He does not silence fear by the idea of annihilation, or absorption, or eternal sleep; but still less by the hope of eternal life after death. Death draws near to the Confucianist solemn, terrific, and alone.

"*Nor bring again the pleasures of past years.*"

There is no hope of "the restitution of all things" in Confucianism. Even ancestral worship, which produces loudly a belief in the continued life of the soul after death, gives no glimpse of resurrection and conscious reunion with the departed. The hope of the most enlightened heathen is indeed but despair. "The whole system of Confucianism offers no comfort to ordinary mortals either in life or death."* Yet this is for China the religion of "the *Truth*."

II.—BUDDHISM.

"Like as the wind is, such is human life,
A moan, a sob, a sigh, a storm, a strife."
Light of Asia.

"Thy saving health among all nations."—*Psalm* lxvii. 3.

Buddhism I must treat in the same summary manner, not attempting to analyse or describe at length its philosophy and history; but merely mentioning some of its salient features as affecting its claim to be one of China's religions.

Buddhism takes the second place in a Chinaman's threefold code of religion: Confucianism, Buddhism and Taoism. Essentially a foreign creed, and introduced from abroad seventeen centuries and more ago, it claims our interest and admiration as a great missionary enterprise which, though now in decay, and destined to eclipse by the uprising of the Light of the World, yet, as *a* light in Asia's darkness, has exercised an influence of well-nigh unparalleled magnitude. This creed is interesting also as depriving the Chinese of their argument against Christianity from the fact of its appearing as a foreign religion. If the Chinese can receive and profess an avowedly foreign creed like Buddhism with foreign objects of worship ridiculed by their own great Emperors K'ang-hyi and

* Faber's "Digest of Confucian Doctrine."

Yung-ching; if they can welcome and eagerly consume the foreign smoke of opium, though denounced by the moral voice of the land, and resisted to the very blood by China's fleets and armies,—how can they reject, unheard and untasted, a doctrine which comes originally not from the West but from Heaven itself; and a creed which is not poison, but the very bread and wine of the soul?

This great religion of Buddhism has, when analysed, no more right than Confucianism to be called a religion at all. Buddhism is avowedly atheistic, setting *Dharma*, or Law, above all gods and goddesses; and giving man the hope of salvation without the intervention of God. Yet Buddhism as well as Confucianism affords in its history a fresh evidence of the irresistible tendency of the human heart to *worship*. Buddha, the Teacher, is now Amidabha, the God. Buddha's temples are crowded with idols. Kwanying, now the Goddess of Mercy (for twelve centuries the God of Mercy), is more popular than Buddha himself, being in fact one of his avâtars.*

Just so in Christendom, the shrine of the Virgin Mary in many Roman Catholic Churches is far more frequented than the shrine of the Divine Saviour. "It was, indeed, a strange irony of fate," remarks Sir M. Monier-Williams, "that the man who denied any God or any being higher than himself and told his followers to look to themselves alone for salvation, should not only have been deified and wor-

* "The word avâtara means the incarnation or rather the descent of some Divine Being."—*Cf.* Monier-Williams' "Buddhism," p. 165.

shipped, but represented by more images than any other being ever idolized in any part of the world."

Moreover, the Nirvâna of pure Buddhism becomes in Northern Buddhistic teaching a palace of light and joy in the Western heavens. Yet when we search behind these modern additions, we find in the words which I have quoted above the ground and motive and explanation of Buddha's teaching. "He despaired of life," and his remedy was not a "better land," a life to come free from sorrow, change, and death, but rather the "Great Renunciation" of personal identity and conscious existence. Buddha taught that the natural yearning after life is an ignorant blunder. And Taoism speaks in much the same way, "It is the destiny of the living to be finite; so that the desire to prolong life, and to *do away with one's end*, is a misunderstanding of one's destiny." Nirvâna, the "passionless bride, Divine tranquillity," is not conscious joy; neither is it conscious sorrow. It is the "state of a blown-out flame."* Now, if this meant the blowing out and away of all evil passions and lusts, it would be good news indeed. Or if it meant the annihilation of the selfishness of self, that, too, were indeed a gospel. But it means the extinction of individual existence; of all action, will, and consciousness. "Christianity," says Sir M. Monier-Williams, "demands the suppression of selfishness —Buddha demands the suppression of self. In the

* This is the original meaning of Nirvâna.—*Cf.* Monier-Williams' "Buddhism," p. 139.

one the true self is elevated. In the other it is annihilated."

And this, the practical negation of God's action and presence, is Buddha's gospel for man, of whom St. Augustine so truly and nobly says, "Fecisti nos ad TE, Domine; et inquietum est cor nostrum donec requiescat in TE."—"Thou hast made us Lord for Thyself; and our heart is restless till it rests in Thee." And this, the promise of Nirvâna, which only by a refinement of sophistry can be distinguished from the extinction of life and consciousness, is Buddha's gospel for man; of whom Tennyson, in one of his latest poems, sings :—

> "And men have hopes, which race the restless blood,
>   That after many changes may succeed
>   Life, which is life indeed."

Words capable of a manifold interpretation, but most vividly describing the love of life which is inextinguishable in the human heart. And this hope Buddha shatters with the promise of " life which is not life at all."

> "If any say Nirvâna is to cease,
>   Say unto such they lie;
>   If any say Nirvâna is to live,
>   Say unto such they err."

And Buddha, just when dying—it is said after eating too much dried boar's flesh (a story the bathos of which is so startling as hardly to admit of the theory of fabrication, as Sir M. Monier-Williams points out)— spoke thus, " Look not to anyone but yourselves as a refuge. Everything that cometh into being passeth away. Work out your own perfection with diligence; that is, your own cessation of conscious being."

The ordinary Buddhist of the present day thinks little, however, of Nirvâna, because it is beyond his comprehension and reach. The hope of the mass of Buddhist worshippers is to escape one of the eight hells, and to be born and die again, either as human beings on this same earth in a somewhat higher sphere; or by transmigration to enter some other bodily form, and in some other world.

And yet this is for China the "*Religion of the Life.*"

III.—TAOISM.

"There is a way that seemeth right unto a man."
"That THY way may be known upon earth."

"Man, on the dubious waves of error toss'd,
His ship half founder'd, and his compass lost,
Sees, far as human optics may command,
A sleeping fog, and fancies it dry land;
Spreads all his canvas, every sinew plies;
Pants for 't, aims at it, enters it, and dies."
COWPER, *Truth*.

Taoism, which some one has called "Buddhism in a Chinese dress," began much in the same way as Buddhism; not as a religious system, but as a philosophic system of morals. No special object of worship was held up by Lao-tsù, the reputed founder of the religion (B.C. 604). His great principle—not ignoble in conception, though impracticable in operation—was that man, in order to be pure and upright, should not so much set himself to obey law; but that "time should run back and fetch the age of gold;" and that man, getting behind all formulated law, should be moral without effort, constraint, direction, or prohibition.

> "There are who ask not if thine eye
>   Be on them : who in love and truth,
> Where no misgiving is, rely
>   Upon the genial sense of youth.
> Glad hearts, without reproach or blot,
> Who *do thy work*, and *know it not*."
>   WORDSWORTH's *Ode to Duty*.

Was this a far-off dream, backwards and forwards; of Eden in the past, and of "the law of Christ" in the future: the righteousness of the law fulfilled and glorified in the new nature? Some have imagined, and not wholly without reason, that Lao-tsù embodies in his philosophy remains of Divine truth, learnt originally through possible commercial intercourse in Solomon's time between East and West.

Taoism in its early days was indeed notable for pure speculation, rather than for any elaboration of religious ceremonies or rites. The search for the elixir of immortality absorbed the attention of Imperial Taoists 2,000 years ago, notably so in the case of the founder of the Ch'in dynasty, B.C. 202, who burnt the ancient books, and built the great wall of China;[*] and also in the case of the Emperor Wu, in the succeeding Han Dynasty, B.C. 100. And alchemy has been a favourite study of the sect. But speculations of a far deeper and higher nature occur. In the writings of Lieh-tsù (Licius *circa* B.C. 400), whom some

---

[*] See Balfour's "Leaves from my Chinese Note-book," pp. 86, 109.

suppose to be a mere "supposititious personage," but who is generally described as one of Lao-tsù's earliest disciples, speculations of the most interesting character occur; but they are speculations, and no more. Here we have, for instance, an anticipation in ancient days of the profound and absorbing study of the origin of life. "There is Life," says Lieh-tsù, "which is uncreated. The Uncreated alone can produce life. The Uncreated stands alone. His duration can have no end." Again, we have speculations as to what is after death; anticipations, are they, of modern theories with reference to "conditional" existence? In a conversation ascribed to Confucius by this Taoist writer, death is represented as "rest for the virtuous, and a *hiding away* of the bad." "The superior man death brings to rest, the low ones to *submission*." But there is no promise of awaking from the rest for the good; or of emerging from the plunge into the darkness of annihilation for the wicked.

It is difficult to imagine how any professor of such a creed can be cheerful. Yet the phenomenon is not an uncommon one in these latter days. It is said of Harriet Martineau that her faith in the progressive happiness and welfare of mankind (albeit that mankind individually she destined in thought to annihilation) seems to have served her in lieu of every other hope in futurity. She passed her latter years in buoyant cheerfulness, when she mentally consigned herself and her dearest and closest ties on earth to an *everlasting separation*.

Infinitely brighter and more buoyant is the Christian hope—

> "Say not good-night, but in some higher clime
> Bid me good-morning." *

Lao-tsù's future for the soul was absorption into Nature; as Buddha's Nirvâna is absorption into the Absolute. Modern Taoism, therefore, with its many gods of Heaven and Earth; with its Lares and Penates; with its geomancy and necromancy; with its table-turning—(a pencil hanging through a hole in a board suspended over a tray of fine sand being supposed to trace characters in the sand moved by unseen mystic powers),—with its gigantic system of Fung-shuy—"the wind and water" influences which are supposed in lucky or unlucky sites and surroundings to sway the fortunes of the living and dead;—all these are not true Taoism at all. But both the original philosophy and its after-developments afford the Chinese only a "blind leading of the blind" instead of the true "*Religion of the Way.*" †

There is one consideration which still further tends to lift Christianity out of the reach of comparison with some of these religions. It is this. Whereas the whole tendency of modern research is to place the date of the books of the New Testament near to the very time on earth of our Lord Himself, the canonical writings connected with Confucius and Buddha seem to be separated from these great men, be they historical, or be they

---

* *Edinburgh Review*, July, 1890.
† The word *Tao* means *Reason*, *Word*, and the *Way* or *Method*.

mythical, by a formidable hiatus, by long stretches of time, or by doubtful genuineness and authenticity.

The burning of the books by the Emperor Shih Huang-ti (B.C. 213), notwithstanding the current stories as to the recovery of certain copies, seems to loosen one's hold on the sure possession of genuine literature. The Lun yü or "Analects" of Confucius, from which most of the details of his life are drawn, could not, thinks Dr. Legge, have been written by Confucius' immediate disciples, but he believes that it might have been compiled by the disciples of those disciples. Confucius was not specially honoured for 250 years after his death; and it was only in the year A.D. 1 that he was canonized as the "Illustrious Duke Ni; lord of completed praise."

Before our Lord's death it was said by His enemies that "the world had gone after Him." Within a year of the Crucifixion, Stephen was glad to die for his Lord. And soon after this all through Asia Minor Christ was worshipped as God: and the temples of the gods were reported by Pliny to be well-nigh deserted.

With reference to Buddhism, though Buddha was born 500 years before Christ, "there is not a single Buddhist manuscript in existence which can vie in antiquity and undoubted authenticity with the older codices of the Gospels."* The supposed Christian elements in Buddha's life, which have so dazzled and confused many weak-sighted people in recent times, are all of comparatively

* See Eitel's "Lectures on Buddhism."

modern date. The most ancient Buddhist classics contain scarcely any details at all of Buddha's life; and none whatever of these so-called Christian elements. Hardly any of the legends about Buddha can be proved to have been in circulation earlier than the fifth century A.D. A writer in the *Quarterly Review* for April, 1890, noticing Sir M. Monier-Williams great book on Buddhism, and Oldenburg's "Buddha," writes thus, "In the Jataka commentaries, the generally-received life of Gautama Buddha, a document apparently older than Christianity, we notice an entire absence of anything at all like Christian history. It may be truly said that the events in the life of Gautama, so far as we can trace it in an historical sense, present an unbroken series of contrasts to the life of Christ, except in the one particular that he went about preaching."

With reference to Taoism the case is different, but it is noteworthy that the *present* Taoist system was founded by Chang Tao-ling (A.D. 34—157), although Lao-tsŭ was born B.C. 604. One of the most popular Taoist books, "The Book of Rewards and Punishments," dates only from the fifteenth century A.D. The celebrated Tao-Teh-Ching is probably much older—Dr. Legge, indeed, ascribes to it the date B.C. 517. But the remark of a writer in the *Quarterly Review* on the Sacred Books of the East is worthy of consideration. "In those early times a book was seldom or never composed in the shape in which it has come down to us. It was not made, it grew."

This cannot be said of the separate Gospels and

Epistles of the New Testament. That book was made. It was complete by the end of the first century A.D. It was accepted by the Church as canonical before the end of the second century.

I cannot close this cursory review of these three religious systems of China without noticing the high excellence of many of their moral precepts, and the comparatively high tone of their moral code.

Confucius exhorts to self-examination. Talents without a moral basis are, he says, not worthy of consideration. The good man is watchful over his conduct when alone. The "golden rule" is given negatively, and in a measure positively,* for "all men within the four seas" are declared to be "brethren." Confucius showed deep pity for suffering, both in man and beast. He laments over the appalling fact that there exists no holy man; no good man; nobody who loves virtue as he loves beauty or sensual pleasure; nobody who strives to carry out *Tao* or the Ideal Way. Confucius was a humble and teachable, and not a self-asserting man. Buddha and Lao-tsù both reach a higher level still. Confucius could not see his way to reward injury with kindness; for how then, he asks in a puzzled tone, how can I recompense kindness? But Buddha and Lao-tsù launch out more boldly. "The good man should even love the man who is not good, and reward illwill with virtue." Injuries should be recompensed with kindness. (Tao-Teh-Ching, ch. lxiii). "Pity the misfortunes of others, and rejoice at their well-being."

* *Cf.* Faber's "Digest."

And in one word of noblest tone, Lao-tsŭ, if he be the author of the saying, asserts that if he must choose between his life and righteous dealing, he will let go life and hold fast to integrity.*

The final verdict as to these three systems must be, that they supply no Mediator and Redeemer from sin, which meanwhile they do not deny or explain away. They speak much of fear; but they breathe no word of love to the eternal God.† They know of no Regenerator who can restore human nature to its high original, the image of the Creator.

The review which I have given above of the religions of China has been brief and imperfect; but it will suffice, I trust, to leave deeply engraven on the minds of my readers the contrast between the Christian's hope and the despair of the heathen; between the full-orbed light of Christian knowledge, and faith, and hope, and the darkness which may be felt of heathen ignorance and superstition. Surely God *has* been merciful to us in Christendom; He *has* blessed us; He *has* in the face of Jesus Christ caused His face to shine upon us. And why? "That His way may be known upon earth; His saving health among all nations." And wilful or careless neglect of the duty and privilege of spreading the light of the Gospel may withdraw that light from our own souls, and lead to the removal of the candlestick of Gospel light from England's homes, and parishes, and churches.

---

* This saying rather belongs to Mencius.
† See "Present Day Tract." (Dr. Legge.)

CHAPTER VII.

FOUR SCENES IN CHINESE EVANGELIZATION.

I.—LINE UPON LINE.

It is a spring day thirty years ago in Mid-China. The great alluvial plain of San-po, to the north of Ningpo, shone on by the warm sun, and swept by the breezes of spring, is fair and pleasant. The beans are in flower, and the wide breadths of these, one of the staple crops of San-po, make the air fragrant. Large stretches of wheat are in ear; wheat harvest falling at the time of our early hay harvest. Here and there the rice seed-beds shine like patches of emerald. The clover in flower has just been plowed into the half-inundated rice-fields for manure; and these fields are dotted over with labourers breaking up the clods of earth with their heavy hoes. Suddenly there is a shout, and every hoe is thrown down, for the rumour of the arrival of a foreigner in this secluded plain passes from mouth to mouth. The foreigners have just left their boat near Ming-ngoh-dziang, a picturesque town at the foot of lofty hills, where the C.M.S. have now a flourishing school and a small body of Christians under the pastoral care of the Rev. Sing Eng-teh, who lives at Kwun-hae-we, five miles to the northward. Then probably for the first time in their lives these countrymen see with their own eyes the foreigner; feared, disliked, suspected, and yet not without true courtesy welcomed oftentimes on these early exploratory journeys. Probably, I say—for on the dangerous coast hard by, some years previously, a British ship had been wrecked; and the captain's wife had been carried to Ningpo and exhibited in a cage, our good native pastor, Mr. Sing, then but a lad, forming part of the staring crowd outside this lady's prison. Now is this foreigner, they ask, in very deed a white demon—a foreign "imp"? Is he like some mythical being, or one with flesh and blood like us? They crowd round attracted by the Western clothing and paler faces of their visitors. Some handle inquisitively their coats and umbrellas; some shout incoherent questions; some simply stare with open-mouthed inarticulate amazement. Amongst these eager gazers was a husbandman named Kying-ming. "He took his eyes," as he said when describing the scene to me in after-years. He stared and glared; and the overwhelming fascination of the sight in the flesh of the long-rumoured Western strangers rendered him deaf to their voices and absolutely inattentive to their message.

The preaching is over now. The Gospel has been proclaimed. Tracts are distributed to those who can read; and with many bows and farewells, the missionaries embark in their small boat and turn her head westwards towards Yü-yiao by canal, and thence by river to Ningpo. Kying-ming goes back to his work. He picks up his hoe; and as he strikes the clods vigorously to make up for lost time, he shouts to his fellows, in the loud voice which these sea-side San-po men have acquired, his astonishment at the sight which has so stirred the plain to-day. What did the visit mean? Are these the foreigners who brought opium to China, and who extract eyes from the dying and dead? Yet they seemed to wish to be courteous. They were not overbearing or violent. They asked for no money. They brought no wares for sale. They actually distributed good books gratis! Strange fellows are these Western barbarians!

Days pass by. Most of the harvest is over; the wheat is long ago gathered, and the early rice cut and carried. The pleasant days of October have come with cool breezes (though the sun still blazes fiercely above); breezes now sweet everywhere with the scent of the *olea fragrans*. The cotton, which is the second staple of San-po, is ripe, and the fields are full of busy labourers again. Again the word is passed that the foreigners have come. Off runs Kying-ming to gaze once more on the sight which had so fascinated him in the spring. But now he takes his "ears as well as his eyes." He listens as that strange figure opens its lips and talks. Talks! Yes, there can be no mistake about it. He is talking, not Western gibberish, but their own Ningpo speech! That discovery once more engrosses and absorbs the man's thoughts. He hears nothing of the text, the message, the argument, the invitation, the warning. He merely hears, and is amazed to hear, a foreigner talking Chinese.

The discourse comes to an end. The missionary

enters his boat once more; and Kying-ming goes home, astonished and perplexed, but wholly unenlightened and unmoved. Well was it for him, and well for the foreign workers, that they were not content with one visit or two. They were not satisfied with the perfunctory execution of their commission, and the bare heralding of the Gospel. "Line upon line," they felt, "precept upon precept," were necessary. They must go again and seek for Christ's sheep. So in the bright days of early December they were in San-po once more, before the great cold with frost and snow had set in, and when the crops being all off the ground, you can walk across country and avoid many a weary twist and bend in the raised stone pathways. Kying-ming is at hand once more, and now with eyes fixed and ears attentive, and with his heart opened by the Spirit of God to receive the truth, he hears not the language only, but the message of salvation, and he believes in the Lord Jesus Christ.

Many years ago after this event I was preaching myself in that same beloved plain, with Kying-ming as my helper. We had had a day of much discouragement; doors slammed in our faces; careless, frivolous, inattentive hearers; much scoffing and no apparent reception of our message. As day declined, weary and sad, I proposed a walk up the hills overlooking the sea and the plain. As we mounted higher and higher, I spoke to my companion of our discouraging day. "Be of good cheer," he said, "I know this plain well. I was brought to God down there. I was once as deaf and as obdurate as the people seemed to be to-day. But we must go again and again to the same places. I should never have found the Saviour if the missionaries had given up the work in despair at our stupidity on their first visit. My eyes, my ears, my heart were opened one after another; and here I am to-day, helping you, sir, to preach the Gospel. Let us try again to-morrow in God's strength!"

I went down to my boat from that hillside, reproved and cheered by my old friend's autobiography.

II.—Pilgrim Preaching.

In the neighbourhood of Ningpo there are several sacred places to which yearly pilgrimages are made. The most celebrated of these is a hilltop some fifteen miles to the eastward, named Ling Fong. On this hilltop lived and died, or (as the belief is) was translated into the state and rank of Lohan or expectant Buddha, a celebrated man with the surname Keh. He flourished about 1,500 years ago; and on his birthday, the tenth day of the Chinese fourth month (generally coinciding with the early days of our month of May), pilgrimages are made by the people of Ningpo, and from far-distant parts of this province, to climb this rugged hill and worship, and buy charms in the temple on its summit. These charms are a curious feature in Buddhist superstition. They are said to have been invented in their present form, in this very city of Ningpo, about 1,000 years ago. During the Song dynasty Ningpo was stormed and the inhabitants all put to the sword, with the exception of a few hundreds who were saved, so the story runs, by the chief priest of a temple still existing near the south gate of Ningpo. He invited the terrified inhabitants to take refuge in his courtyard, sold them tickets, and set them to their prayers. He then placed a bowl of spring water on the temple roof; and when the bloodthirsty soldiers came in pursuit, by his incantations he so affected the enemy that they could not see the temple; the only appearance was the gleam of falling water, and the only sound the mysterious hum of the Buddhist chant. The refugees were saved; and ever since these prayers have been in high repute. They may be bought at any temple, but those purchased at Ling Fong are the most efficacious. They are largely used in cases of serious sickness, and are then burnt as charms whilst the priest is praying. But their chief use is for the unseen world. They are supposed to supply the spirit with passage money to the place of the departed; and with a competency when that abode is reached. These papers are purchased for fifteen or twenty copper cash (from three farthings to one penny); and some of them are said to be worth in the spirit banks hereafter 1,000 dollars or so, that is £200. The weather, therefore, on Keh's birthday, being generally fine, and the air balmy, the hills being carpeted with flowers, and the country green with the spring crops, a holiday being at all times pleasant, and thousands of dollars procurable at so small an outlay, the day of the Ling Fong festival draws vast crowds to the hills. I have visited the chief temple; and also the smaller branch temples in other places, bearing the same name, and with the same pretensions.

Let me briefly describe the scene at one of these "Little Ling Fong" temples in the year 1865.

It was a perfect May day,—

"The bridal of the earth and sky."

Thick dewdrops hung from leaf and flower as we mounted the hill in the early morning. Azaleas made the hillside red, and westeria in festoons hung over the jutting rocks; roses too abounded, and huneysuckle was budding. Birds were singing, the cuckoo and blackbird reminding me of home. We were accompanied, as we ascended, by a dense crowd; and a thick stream of returning pilgrims met us. Alas! how many of these were the "sweet and virtuous souls" of whom Herbert sings? The people told us that about 10,000 persons visited the little temple on that day. Old women were there, panting and groaning under the exertion of the toilsome climb; some are said to die in the attempt. When we reached the summit we found that it was useless and well-nigh impossible to force our way into the temple; so we stood and preached under the shade of trees near the entrance. Presently one of the priests came out and scowled at us. We spoke to him of the sin of deceiving 10,000 people simply for the lust of gain. "Not 10,000" said he, "*only* 6,000; and it is only once a year!" Suddenly a new actor appeared on the scene; and my equanimity and the thread of my discourse were by him seriously disturbed and broken. A madman ran round us, shouting and brandishing his bill-hook close to my head. Some, however, listened to us and received our tracts, and one man vowed never to climb the hill again on so bad and barren an errand. As we descended the hill, the madman went before us, capering like a wild goat. "Ah," said the catechist, "these poor people are all as mad as he." We preached again in a village at the foot of the hill. A man who had just returned from the short pilgrimage listened attentively, and promised to destroy the charms which he had bought as soon as we had left. We expressed doubts as to his sincerity, and he immediately tore them up before our eyes. The surrender of these charms, and of the Buddhist rosaries is a most decisive proof, especially in the case of women, of the sincerity of applicants for baptism.

III.—Too Late.

Many years ago I was itinerating in the great Sanpo plain with Sing Eng-teh, who is now our senior ordained pastor in charge of the churches in that plain. We had been preaching from early morning, and it was now the late afternoon. We were on the outskirts of a great town with some 20,000 inhabitants. We had visited different parts of this important country town, and were wending our way to our boat.

As I passed a courtyard near the bank of the canal, an old man stood at the entrance; and, saluting him with the usual polite phraseology, "What is your honourable name?" "Have you partaken of your evening rice?" "What is your distinguished age?".

—we were astonished to find that he was 90 years of age, and his wife 88. He courteously accepted our offer to enter the courtyard and talk awhile. Chairs were brought, and the old man sat down and listened. His eldest son was dead. His second son came up to look at us, an old man past 70; and looking older than his father. The whole family, now reaching to the fourth generation, was living in one large courtyard, with separate establishments, but as a family still; and, turning round, I saw the daughters and granddaughters-in-law gazing at me with anything but friendly looks; evidently suspecting me of mischievous intentions towards their aged chief. But the old man himself was more than friendly. He listened eagerly and intelligently to our message. He followed with the utmost interest the narrative of our Lord's birth and life; His miracles of mercy arresting his closest attention. But when the death of shame and of pain followed, he could not restrain his indignant remonstrance. "It cannot be true," he exclaimed; "shame on those wicked men! They ought to have died for Him, not He for them!" We explained carefully to him that that death was necessary for this very reason, that men *are* wicked; and that sin cannot pass unpunished either in the person of the sinner or of his merciful Substitute. But the old man continued his indignant exclamation, "Shame on them! shame on them!"

Then he asked us to go inside, disregarding the scowls and warning gestures of the women. We entered; and there sat the old mother, almost beautiful after her 88 winters; with silver hair, and an intelligent, placid face; active, and busily winding cotton with her own hand, and directing the household. She ordered tea at once; and the daughters-in-law, however unwillingly, obeyed. Then I began to talk to the courteous old lady. She shook her head. "I am deaf," she said. I turned to her husband, and begged him to repeat to his wife what we had been saying to him. "It is of no use," the old man said. "She is stone deaf, and never hears a word we say to her. She has been so for some years past." "Well, *you* try," I said to the catechist who was with me, and who had in those days a stentorian voice, which I have often heard ringing above the hubbub of a Chinese market-place. He tried, but wholly in vain. There sat the old woman, friendly and courteous; and we, with our message of salvation, had reached her *too late*. She could not read. It was hopeless at her age to teach her. The sight was one of most moving pathos. Had we come ten years earlier, it might have been in time. Too late now! Was it possible this side the grave? We turned once more to the old man and entreated him to accept the Saviour's love; and to do all he could, by any means he could devise, to teach his wife and his whole family. I visited him often after this. He lived to the age of 99, and his wife nearly as long. He was never baptized; but he accepted Christian books; and kept continually up his sleeve for use a simple prayer. I cannot but hope that these courteous friends, through God's abounding mercy, may have found entrance to the home above; even as they welcomed the least of Christ's followers to their home below. But I can remember no more moving warning to Christian workers. "Beware, lest you come with your message *too late!*"

IV.—Light at Eventide.

My scene changes now to the southern side of the Ningpo hills. Here the population is so great; and the towns and villages lie so thickly scattered, that it was possible sometimes during the hours of a long day, beginning to preach at 7 a.m. and going on till nightfall, to deliver our message and distribute Christian books in ten or twelve different places, varying in size from, for instance, the city of Tsz-chi, with 30,000 inhabitants, down to little villages of a few hundred souls. One of these busy days was drawing to a close. I told my Chinese assistants that there was time to preach once more before dark; and I proposed to press on to a large village of 2,000 or 3,000 people (Ts'ing-shú-wu) half a mile in front. "Sir," they replied, "is not our commission to every creature? Why should we pass by this little village of Din-wu." I had hardly noticed the place; it was so small. But I gladly yielded to their suggestion; and we entered the courtyard. Here we found several men and women sitting in the open air: the men smoking, the women winding cotton. The yard was crowded with straw ricks, and with noisy pigs and poultry. The poor people welcomed us; and chairs were placed for us to sit on; and soon from three corners of the quadrangle trays, each containing eight or ten cups of scalding tea, were brought out for our refreshment. As soon as I began to speak, an old man came and took a seat just in front of me, holding his hand to his ear, as he was deaf. I spoke in a loud voice, and as simply and clearly as possible. I told him of the Saviour's majesty and glory; and of His love in dying for our sins. When I paused, I asked the catechist to follow, taking up and enforcing what I had said. He did so with admirable clearness and power; and the old man, as he caught from us point after point, clapped his hands in an ecstasy of delight. He told me that he had for many years been anxious about his soul, and about the mysterious future world. He had wandered from temple to temple seeking rest and finding none; rejected and ejected by the priests because he had so little money to offer; and now the news of his being justified freely through the redemption which is in Christ Jesus seemed too good to be true; and he clapped his hands again for joy.

> "We clap our hands, exulting
>   In Thine Almighty favour;
> The love divine, that made us Thine,
>   Shall keep us Thine for ever."

Suddenly I felt a hand on my shoulder, and looking up I saw an old woman standing behind me. "Give it to him!" she said, pointing to the old man. "Lecture him well! He is my brother, and a bad brother he has been indeed! His tongue is never quiet; quarrelling and reviling!" The old man, deaf as he was, knew well enough what his sister was saying, and he looked up with a twinkle in his eye. After long and earnest conversation we left, the old man accompanying us on our way for some little distance, eagerly protesting his faith in this new doctrine, and promising to come on the following Sunday to church at Tsòng-gyiao, some four or five miles distant. He kept his promise, and Sunday after Sunday he appeared with great regularity, and became an earnest and intelligent inquirer. After a while he asked for baptism, and I at once questioned him about his unruly tongue. "Oh!" he said, "that is past cure! It has grown old with me, and I fear that I cannot change." "Well," I replied, "if this is so, you cannot be baptized. Baptism means union with the Lord Jesus Christ and with His Church: and for those who are thus really joined to the Lord by the regenerating power of the Holy Spirit, 'old things pass away,' slowly sometimes and partially, but surely and gradually; old habits, old sins, old tempers must go, and all things must become new." "I will try," he said, and he *did* try; but failed from time to time. "I shall ask your sister about you," I said. I did so, and the old woman shook her head significantly; "He is no better," she said; "his tongue is as bad as ever." Still the old man persevered in keeping Sunday holy; he learnt more about the new religion, and begged for baptism. At last, after several months' delay, as I was calling one day at the Tsòng-gyiao Chapel on my way to the distant country districts, I found my old friend waiting for me. He came forward with eager pleasure. "I have done it," he said; "I think you will baptize me now!" "Well, sit down," I said, "and let me hear your story." He then told me that his younger son, who was a rough young fellow,

F

and not very dutiful to him, had lately come home from Shanghai, with a strong antipathy to foreigners. He was very angry at the idea of his old father following the foreigners' religion. One day this son set a hen on thirteen eggs; while he was out in the fields at work, the old man lifted basket and hen and all into the sunshine under the deep eaves of the house. Presently it came on to blow and rain, and the basket was lifted indoors again. Then the son came in, and they sat down to their mid-day meal. When he had done eating, the old man rose from his chair. Without thinking he stepped back into the basket and broke several of the eggs. His son swore and stormed at his father for his carelessness; "and time was" (said the old man to me) "when I would have given him back oaths and angry words more than he gave me. *But I never moved my tongue.* I felt that I had been careless, although I did not do it on purpose. I knew it would only make matters worse to answer my son; so I asked the Holy Spirit to help me, and, will you believe me, I never moved my tongue." "Enough!" I said. "That is just the kind of thing I wanted to hear. Now we will fix a day for your baptism." And with deep thankfulness to God, I soon after baptized him by the name Simeon.

And indeed "his eyes *did* see God's salvation before he departed in peace." His was a joyful active Christian life, though it lasted only eighteen months. He set himself at once to influence others for God. He brought his relatives and friends to church, and so great was the interest excited by the old man, that I felt obliged to open a new outstation nearer to his home for the sake of the many inquirers to whom eight or ten miles' walk on Sunday was no small difficulty.

One day the catechist called on Simeon; and saw on his wrinkled wrist, actually burnt in with a hot iron, a cross. "What does this mean?" he asked. "Oh," replied Simeon, "it was my own idea. No one suggested it; but my memory is short and I am but a stupid old man. I want to remember my Saviour's love at all times. So I burnt a cross on my wrist to remind me."

Soon after this he was laid low by malarial fever, and died. The catechist who called to see him found him sinking fast; but clear in mind and steadfast in the faith. He gave directions about his funeral; that no idolatrous or superstitious rites should be practised; "for I die a Christian," he said. And to his eldest son who waited on him, he said "Son, if you wish to meet your father again, you will find me in heaven with the Saviour. Follow Christ, as your old father has tried to do."

And so "he departed in peace." The catechist who brought me the news burst into tears. "Simeon is dead!" he said. "He is gone! What *shall* we do! His earnest, whole-hearted zeal for Christ stirred us all up. Alas, that he has left us!"

This happened seventeen years ago. The son became a Christian; and he too is now in Paradise with his father; and the memory of old Simeon is still green and fresh at Ningpo, as of one who was a triumph of God's grace, and a bright example of what even the humblest may do for God's glory. Thank God for these evidences of His power working with us, and confirming His word. Will not those who read these narratives ask God to raise up many more such in Ningpo and all over China, who shall be "workers together with Him," and with us; and that, filled with the Holy Spirit, they may mightily testify to the grace of God?

MOH-TS-IN, C.M.S. STATION ON THE EASTERN LAKE.

CHAPTER VIII.

UNEXPECTED AGENCIES.

It is a fact both solemnising and encouraging that God sometimes takes the work of evangelization out of the hands of the ordinary and normal worker, and—

> " Moves in a mysterious way
> His wonders to perform."

It seems as though He would remind us from time to time emphatically that the excellency of the power is of God and not of man.

"The heavens declare the glory of God;" yet with these ethereal preachers "there is no speech nor language." "Their voices cannot be heard." Even the uprising of the sun in his strength, and his coming forth from his chambers in the East, strikes no audible harmony now from the lips of Memnon.

And by other voiceless, inarticulate preachers God still speaks.

To Judas also was committed the message of salvation and the power of healing; and from his lips the Lord may have caused His own message, "The kingdom of heaven is at hand," to sound as clear and with as rousing tones in the hearts of Jewish hearers as from the lips of St. Peter and St. John.

Let me illustrate these two points from brief narratives of modern evangelization.

I.

The history of the Great Valley and Chu-ki Mission was familiar to the students of missionary literature twelve years ago; but so rapidly do events come one upon the other, and so many are the changes in the great battlefield of the Church, that the origin of that Mission may be forgotten altogether or unknown to my present readers. If only the repetition of the story may lead to more fervent and effectual prayer for the whole of the Chu-ki region, I shall not have written in vain. Since the earlier years of courageous faith, and of valiant testimony for Christ, many clouds of disappointment, and decline, and barrenness have gathered over that Church. Some of the elder Christians have given way to grave inconsistency and to dissension; and more tears than smiles have been bestowed on Chu-ki. Yet the work stands; and of late years it has expanded far beyond its original limits; and we believe that much people will yet be added to the Lord from those beautiful hills. And very special prayer is asked for in connection with the different aspects of the Chu-ki Mission thus briefly described; prayer for "those who have gone far astray like lost sheep;" prayer for those whose "souls cleave to the dust," and who have given way to the temptation of apparent pressing need and work now on Sunday; prayer for those who have "lost their first love," in Great Valley, in Si-dang, and elsewhere; prayer that all Christian workers in Chu-ki be "of the same mind in the Lord ; " and prayer that all through that great region " everyone who names the name of Christ may depart from iniquity," and " adorn the doctrine of God their Saviour in all things."

But how was the Gospel first carried to those comparatively remote regions? Not by itinerating preacher; not by Bible colporteur; not by the distribution of Christian literature and the establishment of hospital or school. The soil was unturned, unploughed, unharrowed, save by the long past T'aip'ing troubles. The name of Jesus had never been heard there. The " beautiful feet " of those who preach the Gospel of peace had never been seen there; when suddenly, unexpectedly, well-nigh miraculously, the time of visitation arrived for Chu-ki.

In one of the smaller suburbs of Hangchow, outside the Periwinkle Gate, we had opened, early in 1877, a humble room for preaching to the passers-by, and for quiet talk with inquirers. This special room was opened in consequence of the energetic and faithful work of a catechist and two Chinese theological students. The room was low and dark; and furnished merely with a small table and some benches; and over the door, almost hidden by the deep eaves, in black letters on a red ground, the words were written, " The Holy Religion of Jesus." The room was opened two or three times a week through January, February, and March, with little or no encouragement. Hardly anyone came in to listen; and our eager hopes seemed wholly disappointed. One morning early in April a man named Chow Pao-yong was hastening along the raised causeway which runs past the door of the chapel. He had been staying with friends near, and had started to go into the city marketing. As he passed our door, there was nothing to attract him. The door itself was shut and bolted; the shutters were up; as it was not the usual day for preaching. But happening to look round as he passed, he caught sight of the new red sign paper over the door, and he read the strange word JESUS. He stood still to read it over again; and as our landlady was standing in the sun next door, Mr. Chow saluted her courteously, and asked her if she could tell him what the religion of Jesus might mean. "I am but a stupid woman," she said, "and though I have heard something about it, I cannot clearly describe to you its meaning. You should go into the city and call on Mr. Tai, the Chinese preacher, and on Mr. Moule, the foreign missionary." Mr. Chow, with his interest aroused, asked the way; and the old woman offered to guide him. She did so, and landed him safely at 10.30 a.m. at Mr. Tai's house. A few words of salutation and inquiry showed Mr. Tai what had brought him there; and with faithful zeal he at once, without circumlocution or vague talk, opened his New Testament and took his guest to the Gospel narrative; reading to him for two hours about the Lord's incarnation, and life, and death, and rising again.

Mr. Chow appeared to drink in the truth there and

then; and at 12.30 the two men called on me; and scarcely waiting for the usual inquiries as to name and age and occupation, Mr. Chow at once repeated to me with singular clearness the leading events in the wonderful life of which he had just heard.

So clear was his narrative that I asked him at once where in previous years he had heard the Gospel.

"Never before," he replied; "never till Mr. Tai read to me out of the Sacred Book." He remained in my house as a guest and diligent student of the Bible for two or three weeks, and then went to his far-distant home in the mountains of Chu-ki with Bible, Prayer-book and hymn-book. He went trembling lest his elder brothers should beat him and revile his faith; but he went also eagerly declaring his heartfelt belief in the Lord Jesus. We committed him to God and to the Word of His grace which was able to build him up. And when he was unable to "hide his light under a bushel," as in his timidity he had proposed to do, and when he felt strengthened and compelled to declare the truth, instead of beating their younger brother, the elder men, together with some nephews and neighbours, sat at his feet hearing the Gospel. Catechists from Hangchow were sent down to help him, and after a few months of instruction and preparation, nineteen men, women, and children were baptized. Subsequently, through God's great blessing on the faithful testimony of some of the Christians, and on the evangelistic work of the Chinese catechists, stimulated also and spread far and wide by violent persecution, the work extended rapidly; and more than 100 were baptized within the first two years.

Christians are now to be found in many parts of the Chu-ki region far beyond the original centre of the work, Great Valley; and in nine or ten places Divine worship is held every Sunday. A native ordained pastor, the Rev. Nyi Liang Ping, cares for the Christians; aided by the visits of Mr. Elwin and the Bishop. But I must not attempt here to follow the chequered history of that Mission, nor to dwell on its present state and on its hopes for the future.

Only observe how powerful was the yet *voiceless* name of Jesus over our chapel door; even as the great sun which shone down on our humble mission-room that April day was eloquent in God's glory, though without "real voice or sound." It surely encourages us to go forth with that name which is above every name on our lips, knowing that there is power in the name alone to arrest and bless. Here in Chu-ki, without any movement or previous preparation, the man was arrested, and we trust brought to God by that name alone; and a great work was begun, which through God's grace shall bear fruit to life eternal.

II.

Many years ago a miserable beggar used to haunt the Kwun-hae-we mission-house in San-po. He repeatedly asked for baptism, but was deferred on account of his notoriously evil life. He succeeded, however, in securing a copy of the New Testament in Chinese, and being able to read, he took it with him on his wanderings, and in each village he would read a verse or two, and then close his book and beg.

The man died in misery by the wayside; we fear without evidence of true repentance. He had passed away from our memories, when his life and character were brought before us again in a remarkable manner.

The catechist in charge of one of our stations at the eastern limit of the San-po plain was preaching one summer afternoon at his chapel door. A man passed by with a pack on his back. He paused when he heard the preacher's voice, and sat down for a few minutes to rest and listen. Then he rose and trudged on, a weary walk of seven miles, across a rugged ridge of hills down into the plain in which the city of Ning-po stands.

He entered a village and took down his pack, displaying his store of silks and threads, needles and looking-glasses, to the women who gathered round. Gossiping with them, he told them of the old man whom he had heard that afternoon preaching at the chapel door in San-po, and how he kept talking of some one whom he called "Jesus." "Jesus!" exclaimed one of the women; "wasn't it about Jesus that the beggar used to read to us some years ago?"

The coincidence struck her so forcibly that she started on foot the next day to San-po to hear from the catechist's own lips what he could tell her about Jesus. The road which she took has often wearied me with the single journey alone; but she went there and back again in one day, a walk of from twelve to fourteen miles in length, and this for several Sundays in succession, and with the grievous hindrance of the cramped feet of a Chinese woman. So earnest was she that she exhibited that sweet proof of true Christian sincerity, namely, a desire to bring others within the sound of the good news. She was baptized, and passed through a long fight of affliction on account of her faith.

III.

The more recent and exceedingly interesting work at Da-zih and other places among the T'ai-chow mountains was commenced by an agency, not so strange, perhaps, as in the instances enumerated above, but still by unexpected means. The rumour reached that village of the existence in far-off Ningpo of a foreign hospital where opium-smokers could be cured of the dangerous and pernicious habit. This rumour had been spread by people who had heard (at some distance from Da-zih) the itinerating evangelist sent down from the Ning-po College into those regions by Mr. Hoare. A young man in this village who had taken to opium-smoking, resolved to go to Ningpo and try this new cure. He went, and was gladly admitted as a patient. During his residence there he daily attended the hospital prayers; and one day, when listening to the reading and exposition of the great and marvellous doctrine of the Atonement, he rose, and there and then avowed his amazement at this Divine truth, and his acceptance of this great salvation. He then wrote to urge his father to come up to Ningpo, that he too might hear this new doctrine. The father came, and (as he told me himself at the time of his baptism) when he entered the hospital doors at Ningpo he overheard the blessed sounds of the Gospel being read by a Chinese Bible-woman in the adjoining waiting-room for women, the window of which was open at the time. The sound came back to him as a long-forgotten voice; for twenty years previously he had been accustomed to visit Shanghai. Whilst there he had heard enough to convince him that idolatry was foolish and wrong; and for twenty years he had given up the worship of idols. He had heard also that "all men have sinned, and come short of the glory of God": and for twenty years he had been uneasy because of his sins. But he had forgotten the blessed tidings of pardon and peace in Jesus Christ; and now the voice struck again on his ears—he accepted Christ Jesus as his Saviour; the son believed with his father; and both of them received the truth in the love of it. Soon after their baptism the younger man accompanied some of the Christians to San-po in order to attend as a visitor the Native Church meeting at Kwun-hae-we. The father meanwhile returned to Da-zih. It was a year of great sickness and mortality; and the poor man was seized with virulent cholera as he reached his own door; and died. A few days later the son returned and found his father dead, and the house sacked by the heathen relatives and neighbours, because they thought the curse of heaven had fallen upon one who had deserted his ancestral faith. Who would have wondered if the young Christian had given way before this sore trial? but, strengthened with might by God's Spirit in the inner man, he held firmly to his faith; and he and evangelists sent down to Ningpo have been used by God in gathering together a church of 100 baptized members, with 60 communicants. A school and a small church have been erected; and an ordained pastor, paid in part by the poor Christians themselves, has been appointed to care for the little flock.

Bishop Moule hopes before long that the man who was baptized with his father as the firstfruits of the Mission, may himself be ordained as their pastor and teacher.

Thus a word on a sign-board, the reading of a beggar by the wayside, and the mere rumour of distant physical help, led, through God's gracious guidance and overruling, to widespread work of conversion.

THE SI-KWÔ-MIAO, A TEMPLE ON THE EASTERN LAKE.

CHAPTER IX.

CHINA OPEN—THE FUTURE.

"The good man lives not for himself but for others, and his life is prolonged by so doing. The more he serves, the more he has wherewith to serve; the more he gives, the richer he becomes."—*Chinese Taoist Philosophy*.

"Oh opportunity! opportunity! It is only the true genius who can take opportunity by the forelock! It is only the sagacious who never miss opportunity. But the next best thing is to repent when the opportunity has gone by. Repentance, followed by capacity to change for the better, will yet enable us to repair our errors at some future time!"
—*Chinese account of the* Opium *War*, translated by E. H. Parker.

THE instances of evangelistic work which I have given in the two preceding chapters, some carried on by ordinary, some by extraordinary agencies, are all drawn from a comparatively small corner of the vast Chinese mission-field, but they are to a great extent typical of work in other parts of the field. They show the accessibility of the people; how both men and women can be reached by the Gospel, and are ready through God's grace to receive the Gospel. They show open doors and barriers removed.

Forty years ago, in some of the districts of northern Cheh-Kiang, to which my experience has been chiefly confined, and to which my narrative refers, Fortune,

CHINESE MANDARIN AND FAMILY.

the energetic and successful botanist and explorer, was obliged to travel disguised as a Chinese gentleman, if he was to travel inland at all. The place has been pointed out to me where he was recognised under his disguise, and where consultations were overheard by him, as to his arrest and exposure, and probable rough treatment.

In Hangchow, where for twenty-five years missionaries have been living and working, and for twenty years with full official recognition, foreign residence was impossible thirty years ago, and travellers were liable to be conducted promptly to the coast. Now all this is changed. *China is open.* In whatever dress you please to adopt, travel and exploration are possible in almost all parts of the land. Disguise is no longer necessary, for the foreigner and his creed are matters of notoriety now.

In his remarkable sermon preached last May before the Church Missionary Society, the Rev. Herbert James speaks of the principle of *gradualness* running through the operations of God in things spiritual as well as in the world physical. He warns us against premature action, which only courts failure. We are told in reports, which are now almost ancient literature, that in the early days of this century doors were shut and ways were not open. China, for instance, even to the eyes of eager Jesuit pioneers, seemed shut in as by brazen walls.

One is disposed sometimes to wonder whether these doors *were* so fast shut as Christians supposed. Inside those walls souls were dying fast—souls as precious and as valuable as souls in this year of grace 1890. Beyond those apparently insurmountable barriers Satan was working his tyrant will as the lord and prince of this world. But that world belonged to Christ, the King of kings, as much 100 years ago as it does now.

Doubtless God is sovereign, and salvation is no one's right. The unevangelised nations are not wronged by *God* at all; for all is of grace, not of debt. But they are grievously wronged by the callous lukewarm Church. And two considerations must, I think, modify our thoughts about the gradualness of God's work, true and sober as Mr. James' reflections are. First of all we reverse the picture given in his sermon, and notice not only that the doors were opened when the Church was awakened, but that the Church was sound asleep when the doors of advance seemed shut and barred. That sleep was *criminal*, not Providential; and the doors might *not have been barred at all, had the Church been awake*. A vivid, loving, yearning persuasion that souls were really perishing beyond those barriers would, I think, have led to their overleaping. And, further, if it be sober and wise to advance into the Soudan now, though it is death to be a Christian there, and though English prestige is not to be relied upon, would it have been quixotic to penetrate into China 100 years ago, ignoring exclusiveness, and braving deportation, persecution, or death?

But I dwell on these points also but for a moment in order to emphasize again the great truth that the time of gradualness seems past. The gates are open. The course is free. The Church, with her treasure, the Word of God, can *run* through China, and well-nigh through the world now.

"Our difficulty," continues Mr. James, "is not so much that which hampered Christian effort at the beginning of the century—it is not so much to find openings, as to find men and women who will enter them." It gives one some idea of the change in China to know that by an Imperial Rescript, dated March 14th, 1890, Chung King, the great commercial capital of the province of Szchuen, a city lying 1,500 miles from the coast, was declared an open port for European merchandise; and that residence and missionary work there, in the far-off heart of China, will henceforth be as legal as in Ningpo and Shanghai.

The fascination of ascending mountains hitherto untrodden by foreign feet; the excitement—no ignoble feeling—of geographical discovery: some unmarked hill range; some unmapped branch of mighty river; some glorious view of mountain-peaks or rolling champaign—these are possibilities now for missionary volunteers in China; but, above all, the wonderful privilege and the solemn responsibility of preaching the Gospel where Christ has never yet been proclaimed.

The presence and work of other societies in such a country as China need in no sense prevent our entering as well, if only the obligations of Christian courtesy, and hearty recognition of God's work by other hands, be observed. Most certainly such work cannot relieve Churchmen from personal responsibility.

The presence, for instance, of the China Inland Mission in the provinces of Szchuen and Yunnan, means merely the attempt to evangelize the whole of France and Spain with some twenty or thirty labourers. Even in the small districts of Chuki (as large as the county of Kent) and T'aichow (as large as a large slice of North Wales), there is room enough and to spare for two societies; much more so in the vast provinces of the Empire.

And acting on this persuasion, the Church Missionary Society has sanctioned an experimental mission to Szchuen with new plans and methods of work, suggested by the Rev. J. H. Horsburgh, formerly connected with the Society's Hangchow Mission.

The fascination of inland China unveiling to our gaze must not however lead to the neglect or abandonment of the thickly-peopled districts near the coast-line. Watch the life of those great cities up and down the coast. T'ientsin—a place of great importance—the port of the capital, the northern terminus of the Grand Canal (as Hangchow is the southern terminus), and destined to rise to the first rank when it forms the northern terminus of China's first trunk railway; Shanghai, the commercial eye of China and of those Eastern seas, with 500,000 Chinese inhabitants, and 15 million speaking nearly the same dialect in the country round; Suchow, and Hangchow, China's "earthly Paradises," with at least a million and a quarter of people between them, and thickly-peopled contiguous districts. Ningpo, with her 400,000 souls, and twice as many more within the amphitheatre of her beautiful hills; and with 10,000 speaking the Ningpo dialect; Shaou-hying, with half a million within her walls, and twice as many in her magnificent and well-watered plain; T'ai-chow, Wen-chow, Fuh-ning; Fuh-chow, with its million inhabitants ashore and afloat in its harbours—barren though that city seems while the country work blooms and blossoms as the rose. Hong-Kong, a small fishing village within the memory of man, now with a quarter of a million Chinese, and a British colony with stately houses climbing past to Victoria Peak; Canton, the great and active metropolis of the south; and so round to Pakhoi; and the entrances to Kwangsi and Western Kwangtung. Shall these great regions be abandoned now that China's heart is open—abandoned because in the past the cities have borne but little fruit? Rather let them be prayed over, and wept over, and worked over again and again till God's time of mercy and of power has come.

> "Miss not the occasion—by the forelock take
> That subtle Power, the never halting time;
> Lest a mere moment's putting off should make
> Mischance almost as heavy as a crime."
>
> WORDSWORTH.

The boat communication between river and canal in many parts of China is made by "pas" or haul-overs, the boats being dragged up the steep incline of mud and sand on one side by windlasses worked by men and boys, assisted by extra ropes pulled by water buffaloes. The boat poises for awhile on the summit of the bank while the fees are wrangled over, or, if there be a custom-house near, while the cargo is being examined. Then a push is given, the tow-ropes are unhitched, and the boat slides rapidly down and rushes into the water below. I have often stayed for hours near the foot of the incline, amidst a fleet of boats waiting for their turn to cross. Sometimes by gentle persuasion, sometimes by vigorous pushing, sometimes by courteous entreaty, the boats in front will make way for the stranger; but oftentimes the obstruction is insurmountable, and patient waiting is the only policy. Then when the boat reaches and touches the foot of the incline there is a rush to secure the towing-ropes; they are lifted up dripping with mud, and with a double noose are hitched over the stem of the boat. Now with shouts and sometimes with a well-timed song they begin to haul. The boat moves, and all goes well on the smooth and easier part of the incline. Suddenly there is a check. The boat has stuck fast and is immovable. The boatmen jump out, and with a dozen or more to help them they put their backs to the boat's side, lever it up, and rock it from side to side. It is moving slightly now, and the shout goes up to the men at the capstan, and to the buffalo drivers, to take it on with a rush; they respond, and with a long pull and a strong pull the boat is hauled up to the summit. If they fail to seize that moment of apparent movement, the boat will settle down again, and the toil and fatigue must be gone through a second time.

This scene illustrates not without force the present state of Missions in China. We have passed after long delay through the stage of obstruction and

THE GLORIOUS LAND. 103

relentless opposition. We have reached, however slowly, some semblance of advance in Mission work. But the progress has been in some places scarcely perceptible. The deadweight of ignorance, superstition and sin continuing for years together seems to have made the Church in some portions of the great field stationary or even sliding back. Now, shoulder to shoulder, Christians, unite for China's good. The country is open. The fields are white for the harvest. There is movement, a sound of a going in the tops of the trees; there is advance and hope. The cry goes up for "a large number of ordained missionaries and lay workers to preach the Gospel throughout the length and breadth of the land; to plant churches; to train and educate native ministers and native agents (without whose co-operation our work must be largely in vain); to create a Christian literature; to engage in and direct the supreme work of Christian evangelization; to travel far and wide distributing books; to lend a strong helping hand in the great work of Christian education, and to exhibit to China the benevolent side of Christianity in the work of healing the sick." * Neglect this opportunity: and for years the Church may have to contend again with opposition and deadness. Respond! O Church of the Living God; seize the opportunity; combine with heart and soul and mind and strength, with loving, self-denying gift, with self-dedication, and whole-hearted sympathy, and the creeping forward march may turn to a run and an onward rush ere

* See "Report of the Shanghai Conference," May, 1890.

long; till the summit is reached and the kingdoms of this world have become the kingdoms of our God, and of His Christ.

"What manner of persons ought we to be in all holy living and godliness, looking for and *hastening* the coming of the day of God?"

CHAPTER X.

ALTER EGO.
A WAKING DREAM.

Romans xv. 1-3.   1 *Cor.* x. 24.

It was the sweet dawn of an April day;
Roused by the early light I musing lay:
When suddenly, how brought I cannot tell,
The mystery of being on me fell.
I was aware of what I could not shun,
Another day with this same self begun.
I woke once more, controlled still and confined
By the straight limits of one soul and mind.
Can I transgress these bounds, and pass at will
Into another's world, yet conscious still?
Thus restless, ill-at-ease, I wished to be
Self, but not all the same identity.
Then changed my waking dream: I saw the day
Break on the hills and towns of Far Cathay.
The nation wakes to conscious life again;
To toil and pleasure, or to tears and pain.
" Having no hope " beneath God's blessed sky,
" Far from the life of God " they live and die.
And shall I fret with hopes beyond the grave?
A " child of God " deem *that* high self a slave?
And if men yearn for wider, vaster sphere,
" Look on the things of others " far and near.
Let self step back and mind another's cares;
Laugh in their laughter, weep your tears with theirs.

Plan for them, and supply each weary head
With thoughts they cannot think, with prayers unsaid.
So spend your ransomed life, that all may hear
The tidings of that Ransom ringing clear.
Or if, recoiling from the task, you plead
Weakness and fear; then in each hour of need,
" Not I," the plea of slavish days, shall be
The glad plea of your days of liberty.
" Not I," to toil, to pray, to strive, to win,
But, by the Spirit's grace, my Lord within.
Now into darkness let " the flame be blown,"*
Not of true self, but selfishness alone!
That " Great Renunciation " shall obtain
Not gloom, but joyfulness; not loss, but gain.
So to the loftiest heights of highest heaven,
And to earth's furthest bounds your life be given:
For man's good and God's glory spend your days,
And rise with fetters loosed to work and praise.

* *Cf.* Chapter VI. on Buddhism.

APPENDIX.

The Chinese nation has a literary language known as the classical "wen-li." This is not a *tongue* at all. It is simply the terse, concise, written language of the country. It is a dead language (says Dr. Williamson) but wonderfully alive, impressive, and powerful. It is the language of proclamations, advertisements, contracts, deeds, correspondence, and newspapers: and it is used in all the transactions of life.

It is the language taught in the schools, and it is the language of the Ancient Classics, as well as of Chinese literature generally.* This language has, so far as we know, never been a living spoken language. It is meant for the eye and not for the ear; for books and not for speech. It can be pronounced indeed; but for intelligent apprehension on the part of the hearers it must be translated by the reader into the colloquial spoken by the audience.

This was the difficult double task which missionaries had to perform in public worship, before the issue of versions of the Bible in Mandarin and other "colloquials"; Mandarin being at once the Court language of China, and in its many forms and modifications the common medium of talk for, some

---

* *Cf. Chinese Recorder*, July, 1890.

say, nearly two-thirds of the population. The lessons had to be studied in the difficult "wen-li," and then translated at sight into the "colloquial." The number of dialects spoken in China cannot be accurately stated. Ten are mentioned as "separate and distinct from each other." But these ten have a large number of widely differing varieties; a broad river, or a range of mountains, suffices oftentimes to divide two different tongues with new sets of particles, pronouns, and phrases, so that 200 will probably be a sober estimate.

www.ingramcontent.com/pod-product-compliance
Lightning Source LLC
Chambersburg PA
CBHW020146170426
43199CB00010B/906